# Treasury of
# BEST-LOVED POEMS

# Treasury of BEST-LOVED POEMS

Edited by Christopher R. Moore

Illustrated by Eleanor Fortescue Brickdale

GRAMERCY BOOKS
NEW YORK • AVENEL

Published by Gramercy Books,
distributed by
Random House Value Publishing, Inc.,
40 Engelhard Avenue
Avenel, New Jersey 07001

Manufactured in Singapore

Library of Congress Cataloging-in-Publication Data
Treasury of best loved poems.
p. cm.
ISBN 0-517-07233-5
1. English poetry. 2. American poetry.
PR1175.T675 1991
821'.008—dc20 91-28330 CIP

8 7 6 5 4

# CONTENTS

# INTRODUCTION

It has been said that poetry defies definition, yet few people will acknowledge that poetry can entertain and delight, that it may offer comfort and inspiration, engender tears as well as laughter. Indeed, a poem may capture a moment of truth or beauty, recall an incident in history, celebrate love, mourn a death, or tell a story.

This book is a treasure chest of the poet's art, arranged chronologically, by poet, from the sixteenth century to the twentieth century. All the well-known poets, William Shakespeare, John Donne, William Wordsworth, John Keats, Emily Dickinson, and William Butler Yeats, among many others, are represented. There are also gems by lesser known but nevertheless talented poets including John Clare, Thomas Moore, Ernest Dowson, and Emily Brontë. All the poems are worthy of being called best-loved, for each has withstood the test of time.

*Treasury of Best-Loved Poems* is illustrated by Eleanor Fortescue Brickdale, a prominent British illustrator, painter, and designer of the early twentieth century. These richly detailed and romantic illustrations clearly demonstrate why her work was so esteemed and illuminate most wonderfully the timeless quality of the poetry.

CHRISTOPHER R. MOORE

New York
1991

## THEY FLEE FROM ME

They flee from me, that sometime did me seek,
With naked foot stalking in my chamber.
I have seen them, gentle, tame, and meek,
That now are wild, and do not remember
That sometime they put themselves in danger
To take bread at my hand; and now they range,
Busily seeking with a continual change.

Thanked be Fortune it hath been otherwise,
Twenty times better; but once in special,
In thin array, after a pleasant guise,
When her loose gown from her shoulders did fall,
And she me caught in her arms long and small,
And therewith all sweetly did me kiss
And softly said, "Dear heart, how like you this?"
It was no dream, I lay broad waking.
But all is turned, thorough my gentleness,
Into a strange fashion of forsaking;
And I have leave to go, of her goodness,
And she also to use newfangleness.
But since that I so kindely am served,
I fain would know what she hath deserved.

Sir Thomas Wyatt

## MY TRUE LOVE HATH MY HEART

My true love hath my heart, and I have his,
By just exchange one for another given:
I hold his dear, and mine he cannot miss,
There never was a better bargain driven:
  My true love hath my heart, and I have his.

His heart in me keeps him and me in one,
My heart in him his thoughts and senses guides:
He loves my heart, for once it was his own,
I cherish his because in me it bides:
  My true love hath my heart, and I have his.

Sir Philip Sidney

## THE PASSIONATE SHEPHERD TO HIS LOVE

Come live with me and be my love,
And we will all the pleasures prove
That hills and valleys, dales and fields,
Or woods and steepy mountains yields.

And we will sit upon the rocks
Seeing the shepherds feed their flocks,
By shallow rivers, to whose falls
Melodious birds sing madrigals.

And I will make thee beds of roses
And a thousand fragrant posies,
A cap of flowers, and a kirtle
Embroidered all with leaves of myrtle;

A gown made of the finest wool,
Which from our pretty lambs we pull;
Fair linéd slippers for the cold,
With buckles of the purest gold;

A belt of straw and ivy buds
With coral clasps and amber studs:
And if these pleasures may thee move,
Come live with me and be my love.

The shepherd swains shall dance and sing
For thy delight each May morning:
If these delights thy mind may move,
Then live with me and be my love.

CHRISTOPHER MARLOWE

## A MORNING SONG

*From Cymbeline*

Hark, hark! the lark at heaven's gate sings,
And Phoebus 'gins arise,
His steeds to water at those springs
On chaliced flowers that lies;
And winking Mary-buds begin
To ope their golden eyes:
With every thing that pretty bin,
My lady sweet, arise:
Arise, arise!

William Shakespeare

EFB

## SONNETS

### 12

When I do count the clock that tells the time,
And see the brave day sunk in hideous night;
When I behold the violet past prime,
And sable curls, all silvered o'er with white;
When lofty trees I see barren of leaves,
Which erst from heat did canopy the herd,
And summer's green all girded up in sheaves,
Borne on the bier with white and bristly beard,
Then of thy beauty do I question make,
That thou among the wastes of time must go,
Since sweets and beauties do themselves forsake
And die as fast as they see others grow;
And nothing 'gainst time's scythe can make defense
Save breed, to brave him when he takes thee hence.

### 18

Shall I compare thee to a summer's day?
Thou art more lovely and more temperate:
Rough winds do shake the darling buds of May,
And summer's lease hath all too short a date:
Sometimes too hot the eye of heaven shines,
And often is his gold complexion dimmed;
And every fair from fair sometime declines,
By chance or nature's changing course untrimmed;
But thy eternal summer shall not fade,
Nor lose possession of that fair thou ow'st;
Nor shall death brag thou wander'st in his shade,
When in eternal lines to time thou grow'st:
So long as men can breathe, or eyes can see,
So long lives this, and this gives life to thee.

## 29

When, in disgrace with fortune and men's eyes,
I all alone beweep my outcast state,
And trouble deaf heaven with my bootless cries,
And look upon myself, and curse my fate,
Wishing me like to one more rich in hope,
Featured like him, like him with friends possessed,
Desiring this man's art and that man's scope,
With what I most enjoy contented least;
Yet in these thoughts myself almost despising,
Haply I think on thee—and then my state,
Like to the lark at break of day arising
From sullen earth, sings hymns at heaven's gate;
For thy sweet love remembered such wealth brings
That then I scorn to change my state with kings.

## 55

Not marble, nor the gilded monuments
Of princes, shall outlive this powerful rhyme;
But you shall shine more bright in these contents
Than unswept stone, besmeared with sluttish time.
When wasteful war shall statues overturn,
And broils root out the work of masonry,
Nor Mars his sword nor war's quick fire shall burn
The living record of your memory.
'Gainst death and all-oblivious enmity
Shall you pace forth; your praise shall still find room
Even in the eyes of all posterity
That wear this world out to the ending doom.
So, till the judgment that yourself arise,
You live in this, and dwell in lovers' eyes.

## 116

Let me not to the marriage of true minds
Admit impediments. Love is not love
Which alters when it alteration finds,
Or bends with the remover to remove:
Oh, no! it is an ever-fixéd mark,
That looks on tempests and is never shaken;
It is the star to every wandering bark,
Whose worth's unknown, although his height be taken.
Love's not Time's fool, though rosy lips and cheeks
Within his bending sickle's compass come;
Love alters not with his brief hours and weeks,
But bears it out even to the edge of doom.
If this be error and upon me proved,
I never writ, nor no man ever loved.

## 130

My mistress' eyes are nothing like the sun;
Coral is far more red than her lips' red;
If snow be white, why then her breasts are dun;
If hairs be wires, black wires grow on her head.
I have seen roses damasked, red and white,
But no such roses see I in her cheeks;
And in some perfumes is there more delight
Than in the breath that from my mistress reeks.
I love to hear her speak, yet well I know
That music hath a far more pleasing sound;
I grant I never saw a goddess go;
My mistress, when she walks, treads on the ground.
And yet, by heaven, I think my love as rare
As any she belied with false compare.

William Shakespeare

## MY SWEETEST LESBIA

My sweetest Lesbia, let us live and love,
And though the sager sort our deeds reprove,
Let us not weigh them. Heaven's great lamps do dive
Into their west, and straight again revive,
But soon as once set is our little light,
Then must we sleep one ever-during night.

If all would lead their lives in love like me,
Then bloody swords and armor should not be;
No drum nor trumpet peaceful sleeps should move,
Unless alarm came from the camp of love.
But fools do live, and waste their little light,
And seek with pain their ever-during night.

When timely death my life and fortune ends,
Let not my hearse be vexed with mourning friends,
But let all lovers, rich in triumph, come
And with sweet pastimes grace my happy tomb;
And Lesbia, close up thou my little light,
And crown with love my ever-during night.

THOMAS CAMPION

EFB

# THE CHARACTER OF A HAPPY LIFE

How happy is he born and taught
    That serveth not another's will,
Whose armor is his honest thought,
    And simple truth his utmost skill!

Whose passions not his masters are,
    Whose soul is still prepared for death,
Untied unto the world by care
    Of public fame or private breath;

Who envies none that chance doth raise,
    Nor vice; who never understood
How deepest wounds are given by praise;
    Nor rules of state, but rules of good;

Who hath his life from rumors freed,
    Whose conscience is his strong retreat,
Whose state can neither flatterers feed,
    Nor ruin make oppressors great;

Who God doth late and early pray
    More of his grace than gifts to lend,
And entertains the harmless day
    With a religious book or friend.

This man is freed from servile bands
    Of hope to rise or fear to fall:
Lord of himself, though not of lands,
    And, having nothing, yet hath all.

Sir Henry Wotton

## DEATH BE NOT PROUD

Death, be not proud, though some have callèd thee
Mighty and dreadful, for thou art not so:
For those whom thou think'st thou dost overthrow
Die not, poor Death; nor yet canst thou kill me.
From Rest and Sleep, which but thy picture be,
Much pleasure, then from thee much more must flow;
And soonest our best men with thee do go—
Rest of their bones and souls' delivery!
Thou'rt slave to fate, chance, kings, and desperate men,
And dost with poison, war, and sickness dwell;
And poppy or charms can make us sleep as well
And better than thy stroke. Why swell'st thou then?
One short sleep past, we wake eternally,
And Death shall be no more: Death, thou shalt die!

John Donne

EFB

## SONG

Go and catch a falling star,
  Get with child a mandrake root,
Tell me where all past years are,
  Or who cleft the devil's foot;
Teach me to hear mermaids singing,
Or to keep off envy's stinging,
        And find
        What wind
Serves to advance an honest mind.

If thou be'st born to strange sights,
  Things invisible to see,
Ride ten thousand days and nights
  Till Age snow white hairs on thee;
Thou, when thou return'st, wilt tell me
All strange wonders that befell thee,
        And swear
        No where
Lives a woman true and fair.

If thou find'st one, let me know;
  Such a pilgrimage were sweet.
Yet do not; I would not go,
  Though at next door we might meet.
Though she were true when you met her,
And last, till you write your letter,
        Yet she
        Will be
False, ere I come, to two or three.

JOHN DONNE

## ON MY FIRST SON

Farewell, thou child of my right hand, and joy;
My sin was too much hope of thee, loved boy:
Seven years thou'wert lent to me, and I thee pay,
Exacted by thy fate, on the just day.
O could I lose all father now! for why
Will man lament the state he should envy,
To have so soon 'scaped world's and flesh's rage,
And, if no other misery, yet age?
Rest in soft peace, and asked, say, "Here doth lie
Ben Jonson his best piece of poetry."
For whose sake henceforth all his vows be such
As what he loves may never like too much.

BEN JONSON

## TO CELIA

Drink to me only with thine eyes,
  And I will pledge with mine;
Or leave a kiss but in the cup
  And I'll not look for wine.
The thirst that from the soul doth rise
  Doth ask a drink divine;
But might I of Jove's nectar sup,
  I would not change for thine.

I sent thee late a rosy wreath,
  Not so much honoring thee
As giving it a hope that there
  It could not withered be;
But thou thereon didst only breathe,
  And sent'st it back to me;
Since when it grows, and smells, I swear,
  Not of itself but thee!

BEN JONSON

## TO THE VIRGINS TO MAKE MUCH OF TIME

Gather ye rosebuds while ye may,
  Old Time is still a-flying:
And this same flower that smiles today,
  Tomorrow will be dying.

The glorious lamp of heaven, the Sun,
  The higher he's a-getting
The sooner will his race be run,
  And nearer he's to setting.

That age is best which is the first,
  When youth and blood are warmer;
But being spent, the worse, and worst
  Times, still succeed the former.

Then be not coy, but use your time;
  And while ye may, go marry:
For having lost but once your prime,
  You may for ever tarry.

Robert Herrick

## TO ANTHEA, WHO MAY COMMAND HIM ANYTHING

Bid me to live, and I will live
  Thy protestant to be:
Or bid me love, and I will give
  A loving heart to thee.

A heart as soft, a heart as kind,
  A heart as sound and free
As in the whole world thou canst find,
  That heart I'll give to thee.

Bid that heart stay, and it will stay,
  To honor thy decree:
Or bid it languish quite away,
  And 't shall do so for thee.

Bid me to weep, and I will weep
  While I have eyes to see:
And having none, yet I will keep
  A heart to weep for thee.

Bid me despair, and I'll despair,
  Under that cypress tree:
Or bid me die, and I will dare
  E'en Death, to die for thee.

Thou art my life, my love, my heart,
  The very eyes of me,
And hast command of every part,
  To live and die for thee.

ROBERT HERRICK

## THE PULLEY

When God at first made man,
Having a glass of blessings standing by,
"Let us," said he, "pour on him all we can.
Let the world's riches, which disperséd lie,
Contract into a span."

So strength first made a way;
Then beauty flowed, then wisdom, honor, pleasure.
When almost all was out, God made a stay,
Perceiving that, alone of all his treasure,
Rest in the bottom lay.

"For if I should," said he,
"Bestow this jewel also on my creature,
He would adore my gifts instead of me,
And rest in Nature, not the God of Nature;
So both should losers be.

"Yet let him keep the rest,
But keep them with repining restlessness.
Let him be rich and weary, that at least,
If goodness lead him not, yet weariness
May toss him to my breast."

GEORGE HERBERT

## ON HIS BLINDNESS

When I consider how my light is spent
'Ere half my days in this dark world and wide,
And that one talent which is death to hide
Lodged with me useless, though my soul more bent
To serve therewith my Maker, and present
My true account, lest He returning chide;

"Doth God exact day-labor, light denied?"
I fondly ask. But Patience, to prevent
That murmur, soon replies, "God doth not need
Either man's work or his own gifts. Who best
Bear His mild yoke, they serve Him best. His state
Is kingly: thousands at His bidding speed,
And post o'er land and ocean without rest;
They also serve who only stand and wait."

John Milton

## WHY SO PALE AND WAN

Why so pale and wan, fond lover?
Prithee, why so pale?
Will, when looking well can't move her,
Looking ill prevail?
Prithee, why so pale?

Why so dull and mute, young sinner?
Prithee, why so mute?
Will, when speaking well can't win her,
Saying nothing do 't?
Prithee, why so mute?

Quit, quit for shame! This will not move;
This cannot take her.
If of herself she will not love,
Nothing can make her.
The devil take her!

Sir John Suckling

## TO MY DEAR AND LOVING HUSBAND

If ever two were one, then surely we.
If ever man were lov'd by wife, then thee.
If ever wife was happy in a man,
Compare with me, ye women, if you can.
I prize thy love more than whole Mines of gold,
Or all the riches that the East doth hold.
My love is such that Rivers cannot quench,
Nor ought but love from thee give recompence.
Thy love is such I can no way repay;
The heavens reward thee manifold I pray.
Then while we live, in love lets so persever,
That when we live no more, we may live ever.

ANNE BRADSTREET

E.F.B.

## TO ALTHEA FROM PRISON

When Love with unconfinèd wings
  Hovers within my gates,
And my divine Althea brings
  To whisper at the grates;
When I lie tangled in her hair
  And fetter'd to her eye,
The birds that wanton in the air
  Know no such liberty.

When flowing cups run swiftly round
  With no allaying Thames,
Our careless heads with roses crown'd,
  Our hearts with loyal flames;
When thirsty grief in wine we steep,
  When healths and draughts go free,
Fishes that tipple in the deep
  Know no such liberty.

When, like committed linnets, I
  With shriller voice shall sing
The sweetness, mercy, majesty
  And glories of my King;
When I shall voice aloud, how good
  He is, how great should be,
Enlargéd winds that curl the flood
  Know no such liberty.

Stone walls do not a prison make,
  Nor iron bars a cage;
Minds innocent and quiet take
  That for an hermitage;
If I have freedom in my love
  And in my soul am free,
Angels alone, that soar above,
  Enjoy such liberty.

RICHARD LOVELACE

## SOLITUDE

Happy the man, whose wish and care
A few paternal acres bound,
Content to breathe his native air
        In his own ground.

Whose herds with milk, whose fields with bread,
Whose flocks supply him with attire;
Whose trees in summer yield him shade,
        In winter, fire.

Blest, who can unconcernedly find
Hours, days, and years slide soft away
In health of body, peace of mind;
        Quiet by day.

Sound sleep by night; study and ease
Together mixed, sweet recreation,
And innocence, which most does please
        With meditation.

Thus let me live, unseen, unknown;
Thus unlamented let me die,
Steal from the world, and not a stone
        Tell where I lie.

ALEXANDER POPE

EFB

## ELEGY WRITTEN IN A COUNTRY CHURCHYARD

The curfew tolls the knell of parting day,
The lowing herd wind slowly o'er the lea,
The ploughman homeward plods his weary way,
And leaves the world to darkness and to me.

Now fades the glimmering landscape on the sight,
And all the air a solemn stillness holds,
Save where the beetle wheels his droning flight,
And drowsy tinklings lull the distant folds:

Save where from yonder ivy-mantled tower
The moping owl does to the moon complain
Of such as, wandering near her secret bower,
Molest her ancient solitary reign.

Beneath those rugged elms, that yew tree's shade
Where heaves the turf in many a moldering heap,
Each in his narrow cell for ever laid,
The rude forefathers of the hamlet sleep.

The breezy call of incense-breathing morn,
The swallow twittering from the straw-built shed,
The cock's shrill clarion, or the echoing horn,
No more shall rouse them from their lowly bed.

For them no more the blazing hearth shall burn,
Or busy housewife ply her evening care:
No children run to lisp their sire's return,
Or climb his knees the envied kiss to share.

Oft did the harvest to their sickle yield,
Their furrow oft the stubborn glebe has broke;
How jocund did they drive their team afield!
How bowed the woods beneath their sturdy stroke!

Let not ambition mock their useful toil,
Their homely joys, and destiny obscure;
Nor grandeur hear with a disdainful smile
The short and simple annals of the poor.

The boast of heraldry, the pomp of power,
And all that beauty, all that wealth e'er gave
Awaits alike th' inevitable hour:—
The paths of glory lead but to the grave.

Nor you, ye proud, impute to these the fault,
If memory o'er their tomb no trophies raise,
Where through the long-drawn aisle and fretted vault
The pealing anthem swells the note of praise.

Can storied urn or animated bust
Back to its mansion call the fleeting breath?
Can honor's voice provoke the silent dust,
Or flattery soothe the dull, cold ear of death?

Perhaps in this neglected spot is laid
Some heart once pregnant with celestial fire;
Hands, that the rod of empire might have swayed,
Or waked to ecstasy the living lyre.

But knowledge to their eyes her ample page,
Rich with the spoils of time, did ne'er unroll;
Chill penury repressed their noble rage,
And froze the genial current of the soul.

Full many a gem of purest ray serene
The dark unfathomed caves of ocean bear:
Full many a flower is born to blush unseen,
And waste its sweetness on the desert air.

Some village-Hampden, that with dauntless breast
The little tyrant of his fields withstood;
Some mute inglorious Milton here may rest,
Some Cromwell, guiltless of his country's blood.

Th' applause of listening senates to command,
The threats of pain and ruin to despise,
To scatter plenty o'er a smiling land,
And read their history in a nation's eyes,

Their lot forbade: nor circumscribed alone
Their growing virtues, but their crimes confined;
Forbade to wade through slaughter to a throne,
And shut the gates of mercy on mankind;

The struggling pangs of conscious truth to hide,
To quench the blushes of ingenuous shame,
Or heap the shrine of luxury and pride
With incense kindled at the Muse's flame.

Far from the madding crowd's ignoble strife,
Their sober wishes never learned to stray;
Along the cool sequestered vale of life
They kept the noiseless tenor of their way.

Yet e'en these bones from insult to protect
Some frail memorial still erected nigh,
With uncouth rhymes and shapeless sculpture decked
Implores the passing tribute of a sigh.

Their name, their years, spelt by th' unlettered Muse,
The place of fame and elegy supply:
And many a holy text around she strews,
That teach the rustic moralist to die.

For who, to dumb forgetfulness a prey,
This pleasing anxious being e'er resigned,
Left the warm precincts of the cheerful day,
Nor cast one longing, lingering look behind?

On some fond breast the parting soul relies,
Some pious drops the closing eye requires;
E'en from the tomb the voice of Nature cries,
E'en in our ashes live their wonted fires.

For thee, who, mindful of th' unhonored dead,
Dost in these lines their artless tale relate;
If chance, by lonely contemplation led,
Some kindred spirit shall enquire thy fate

Haply some hoary-headed swain may say,
"Oft have we seen him at the peep of dawn
Brushing with hasty steps the dews away,
To meet the sun upon the upland lawn;

"There at the foot of yonder nodding beech
That wreathes its old fantastic roots so high,
His listless length at noon-tide would he stretch,
And pore upon the brook that babbles by.

"Hard by yon wood, now smiling as in scorn,
Muttering his wayward fancies he would rove;
Now drooping woeful-wan, like one forlorn,
Or crazed with care, or crossed in hopeless love.

"One morn I missed him on the customed hill,
Along the heath, and near his favorite tree;
Another came; nor yet beside the rill,
Nor up the lawn, nor at the wood was he;

"The next, with dirges due in sad array
Slow through the church-way path we saw him borne—
Approach and read (for thou canst read) the lay
Graved on the stone beneath yon aged thorn."

THE EPITAPH

*Here rests his head upon the lap of earth*
*A youth, to fortune and to fame unknown;*
*Fair science frowned not on his humble birth*
*And melancholy marked him for her own.*

*Large was his bounty, and his soul sincere;*
*Heaven did a recompense as largely send:*
*He gave to misery all he had, a tear;*
*He gained from heaven ('twas all he wished) a friend.*

*No farther seek his merits to disclose,*
*Or draw his frailties from their dread abode*
*(There they alike in trembling hope repose),*
*The bosom of his Father and his God.*

THOMAS GRAY

## WHEN LOVELY WOMAN STOOPS TO FOLLY

When lovely woman stoops to folly,
And finds too late that men betray,
What charm can soothe her melancholy,
What art can wash her guilt away?

The only art her guilt to cover,
To hide her shame from every eye,
To give repentance to her lover,
And wring his bosom—is to die.

Oliver Goldsmith

## TO THE EVENING STAR

Thou fair-haired angel of the evening,
Now, whilst the sun rests on the mountains, light
Thy bright torch of love; thy radiant crown
Put on, and smile upon our evening bed!
Smile on our loves, and, while thou drawest the
Blue curtains of the sky, scatter thy silver dew
On every flower that shuts its sweet eyes
In timely sleep. Let thy west wind sleep on
The lake; speak silence with thy glimmering eyes,
And wash the dusk with silver. Soon, full soon,
Dost thou withdraw; then the wolf rages wide,
And the lion glares through the dun forest:
The fleeces of our flocks are covered with
Thy sacred dew: protect them with thine influence.

William Blake

## INTRODUCTION TO SONGS OF INNOCENCE

Piping down the valleys wild,
Piping songs of pleasant glee,
On a cloud I saw a child,
And he laughing said to me:

"Pipe a song about a Lamb!"
So I piped with merry cheer.
"Piper, pipe that song again";
So I piped: he wept to hear.

"Drop thy pipe, thy happy pipe;
Sing thy songs of happy cheer";
So I sang the same again,
While he wept with joy to hear.

"Piper, sit thee down and write
In a book, that all may read."
So he vanished from my sight,
And I plucked a hollow reed,

And I made a rural pen,
And I stained the water clear,
And I wrote my happy songs
Every child may joy to hear.

WILLIAM BLAKE

## THE LAMB

Little Lamb, who made thee?
  Dost thou know who made thee;
Gave thee life and bid thee feed
By the stream and o'er the mead;
Gave thee clothing of delight,
Softest clothing, woolly, bright;
Gave thee such a tender voice
Making all the vales rejoice?
  Little Lamb, who made thee?
  Dost thou know who made thee?

  Little Lamb, I'll tell thee,
  Little Lamb, I'll tell thee:
He is called by thy name,
For He calls Himself a Lamb.
He is meek and He is mild;
He became a little child.
I a child and thou a lamb,
We are called by His name.
  Little Lamb, God bless thee.
  Little Lamb, God bless thee.

WILLIAM BLAKE

## THE TYGER

Tyger! Tyger! burning bright
In the forests of the night,
What immortal hand or eye
Could frame thy fearful symmetry?

In what distant deeps or skies
Burnt the fire of thine eyes?
On what wings dare he aspire?
What the hand dare seize the fire?

And what shoulder, and what art,
Could twist the sinews of thy heart?
And when thy heart began to beat,
What dread hand? and what dread feet?

What the hammer? what the chain?
In what furnace was thy brain?
What the anvil? what dread grasp
Dare its deadly terrors clasp?

When the stars threw down their spears
And watered heaven with their tears,
Did he smile his work to see?
Did he who made the Lamb make thee?

Tyger! Tyger! burning bright
In the forests of the night,
What immortal hand or eye
Dare frame thy fearful symmetry?

William Blake

## TO A MOUSE

*On Turning Her Up in Her Nest with the Plough,*
*November 1755*

Wee, sleekit, cowrin, tim'rous beastie,
O, what a panic's in thy breastie!
Thou need na start awa sae hasty,
    Wi' bickering brattle!
I wad be laith to rin an' chase thee,
    Wi' murd'ring pattle!

I'm truly sorry man's dominion,
Has broken nature's social union,
An' justifies that ill opinion,
    Which makes thee startle
At me, thy poor, earth-born companion,
    An' fellow-mortal!

I doubt na, whiles, but thou may thieve;
What then? poor beastie, thou maun live!
A daimen icker in a thrave
    'S a sma' request;
I'll get a blessin wi' the lave,
    An' never miss't!

Thy wee bit housie, too, in ruin!
It's silly wa's the winds are strewin!
An' naething, now, to build a new ane,
    O' foggage green!
An' bleak December's winds ensuin,
    Baith snell an' keen!

Thou saw the fields laid bare an' waste,
An' weary winter comin' fast,
An' cozie here, beneath the blast,
Thou thought to dwell—
Till crash! the cruel coulter past
Out thro' thy cell.

That wee bit heap o'leaves an' stibble,
Has cost thee mony a weary nibble!
Now thou's turned out, for a' thy trouble,
But house or hald,
To thole the winter's sleety dribble,
An' cranreuch cauld!

But, Mousie, thou art no thy lane,
In proving foresight may be vain;
The best-laid schemes o' mice an' men
Gang aft agley,
An' lea'e us nought but grief an' pain
For promised joy!

Still thou art blest, compared wi' me;
The present only toucheth thee:
But och! I backward cast my e'e,
On prospects drear!
An' forward, tho' I canna see,
I guess an' fear!

Robert Burns

## A RED, RED ROSE

O my Luve's like a red, red rose
  That's newly sprung in June:
O my Luve's like the melodie
  That's sweetly play'd in tune!

As fair art thou, my bonnie lass,
  So deep in luve am I:
And I will luve thee still, my dear,
  Till a' the seas gang dry:

Till a' the seas gang dry, my dear,
  And the rocks melt wi' the sun;
I will luve thee still, my dear,
  While the sands o' life shall run.

And fare thee weel, my only Luve,
  And fare thee weel a while!
And I will come again, my Luve,
  Tho' it were ten thousand mile.

ROBERT BURNS

EFB

## PERFECT WOMAN

She was a phantom of delight
When first she gleam'd upon my sight;
A lovely apparition, sent
To be a moment's ornament;
Her eyes as stars of twilight fair;
Like twilight's, too, her dusky hair;
But all things else about her drawn
From May-time and the cheerful dawn;
A dancing shape, an image gay,
To haunt, to startle, and waylay.

I saw her upon nearer view,
A Spirit, yet a Woman too!
Her household motions light and free,
And steps of virgin liberty;
A countenance in which did meet
Sweet records, promises as sweet;
A creature not too bright or good
For human nature's daily food;
For transient sorrows, simple wiles,
Praise, blame, love, kisses, tears, and smiles.

And now I see with eye serene
The very pulse of the machine;
A being breathing thoughtful breath,
A traveler between life and death;
The reason firm, the temperate will,
Endurance, foresight, strength, and skill;
A perfect Woman, nobly plann'd,
To warm, to comfort, and command;
And yet a Spirit still, and bright
With something of angelic light.

William Wordsworth

# THE DAFFODILS

I wandered lonely as a cloud
That floats on high o'er vales and hills,
When all at once I saw a crowd,
A host of golden daffodils,
Beside the lake, beneath the trees
Fluttering and dancing in the breeze.

Continuous as the stars that shine
And twinkle on the milky way,
They stretched in never-ending line
Along the margin of a bay:
Ten thousand saw I at a glance
Tossing their heads in sprightly dance.

The waves beside them danced, but they
Out-did the sparkling waves in glee:
A poet could not but be gay
In such a jocund company!
I gazed—and gazed—but little thought
What wealth the show to me had brought:

For oft, when on my couch I lie
In vacant or in pensive mood,
They flash upon that inward eye
Which is the bliss of solitude;
And then my heart with pleasure fills,
And dances with the daffodils.

William Wordsworth

## THE RAINBOW

My heart leaps up when I behold
A rainbow in the sky:
So was it when my life began;
So is it now I am a man;
So be it when I shall grow old,
Or let me die!
The Child is father of the Man;
And I could wish my days to be
Bound each to each by natural piety.

William Wordsworth

## SHE DWELT AMONG THE UNTRODDEN WAYS

She dwelt among the untrodden ways
Beside the springs of Dove,
A maid whom there were none to praise
And very few to love:

A violet by a mossy stone
Half hidden from the eye.
—Fair as a star, when only one
Is shining in the sky.

She lived unknown, and few could know
When Lucy ceased to be;
But she is in her grave, and, oh,
The difference to me!

William Wordsworth

# THE WORLD IS TOO MUCH WITH US

The world is too much with us; late and soon,
Getting and spending, we lay waste our powers:
Little we see in Nature that is ours;
We have given our hearts away, a sordid boon!
The sea that bares her bosom to the moon;
The winds that will be howling at all hours,
And are up-gathered now like sleeping flowers;
For this, for everything, we are out of tune;
It moves us not.—Great God! I'd rather be
A pagan suckled in a creed outworn.
So might I, standing on this pleasant lea,
Have glimpses that would make me less forlorn;
Have sight of Proteus rising from the sea;
Or hear old Triton blow his wreathed horn.

William Wordsworth

## COMPOSED UPON WESTMINSTER BRIDGE

Earth has not anything to show more fair:
Dull would he be of soul who could pass by
A sight so touching in its majesty;
This City now doth, like a garment, wear
The beauty of the morning; silent, bare,
Ships, towers, domes, theaters, and temples lie
Open unto the fields, and to the sky;
All bright and glittering in the smokeless air.
Never did sun more beautifully steep
In his first splendor, valley, rock, or hill;
Ne'er saw I, never felt, a calm so deep!
The river glideth at his own sweet will:
Dear God! the very houses seem asleep;
And all that mighty heart is lying still!

William Wordsworth

## IT IS A BEAUTEOUS EVENING

It is a beauteous evening, calm and free,
The holy time is quiet as a Nun
Breathless with adoration; the broad sun
Is sinking down in its tranquility;
The gentleness of heaven broods o'er the Sea:
Listen! the mighty Being is awake,
And doth with his eternal motion make
A sound like thunder—everlastingly.
Dear Child! dear Girl! that walkest with me here,
If thou appear untouched by solemn thought,
Thy nature is not therefore less divine:
Thou liest in Abraham's bosom all the year,
And worship'st at the Temple's inner shrine,
God being with thee when we know it not.

William Wordsworth

## MUTABILITY

From low to high doth dissolution climb,
And sink from high to low, along a scale
Of awful notes, whose concord shall not fail;
A musical but melancholy chime,
Which they can hear who meddle not with crime,
Nor avarice, nor over-anxious care.
Truth fails not; but her outward forms that bear
The longest date do melt like frosty rime,
That in the morning whitened hill and plain
And is no more; drop like the tower sublime
Of yesterday, which royally did wear
His crown of weeds, but could not even sustain
Some casual shout that broke the silent air,
Or the unimaginable touch of Time.

William Wordsworth

# KUBLA KHAN

In Xanadu did Kubla Khan
   A stately pleasure-dome decree:
Where Alph, the sacred river, ran
Through caverns measureless to man
   Down to a sunless sea.
So twice five miles of fertile ground
With walls and towers were girdled round:
And here were gardens bright with sinuous rills,
Where blossomed many an incense-bearing tree,
And here were forests ancient as the hills,
Enfolding sunny spots of greenery.

But oh! that deep romantic chasm which slanted
Down the green hill athwart a cedarn cover!
A savage place; as holy and enchanted
As e'er beneath a waning moon was haunted
By woman wailing for her demon-lover!
And from this chasm, with ceaseless turmoil seething,
As if this earth in fast thick pants were breathing,
A mighty fountain momently was forced,
Amid whose swift half-intermitted burst
Huge fragments vaulted like rebounding hail,
Or chaffy grain beneath the thresher's flail:
And 'mid these dancing rocks at once and ever
It flung up momently the sacred river.
Five miles meandering with a mazy motion
Through wood and dale the sacred river ran,
Then reached the caverns measureless to man,
And sank in tumult to a lifeless ocean:
And 'mid this tumult Kubla heard from far
Ancestral voices prophesying war!

The shadow of the dome of pleasure
Floated midway on the waves;
    Where was heard the mingled measure
    From the fountain and the caves.
It was a miracle of rare device,
A sunny pleasure-dome with caves of ice!

    A damsel with a dulcimer
    In a vision once I saw:
    It was an Abyssinian maid,
    And on her dulcimer she played,
    Singing of Mount Abora.
    Could I revive within me
    Her symphony and song,
    To such a deep delight 'twould win me,
That with music loud and long,
I would build that dome in air,
That sunny dome! those caves of ice!
And all who heard should see them there,
And all should cry, Beware! Beware!
His flashing eyes, his floating hair!
Weave a circle round him thrice,
And close your eyes with holy dread,
For he on honey-dew hath fed,
And drunk the milk of Paradise.

Samuel Taylor Coleridge

## ON AN INFANT DYING AS SOON AS BORN

I saw where in the shroud did lurk
A curious frame of Nature's work;
A floweret crush'd in the bud,
A nameless piece of Babyhood,
Was in her cradle-coffin lying;
Extinct, with scarce the sense of dying:
So soon to exchange the imprisoning womb
For darker closets of the tomb!
She did but ope an eye, and put
A clear beam forth, then straight up shut
For the long dark: ne'er more to see
Through glasses of mortality.
  Riddle of destiny, who can show
What thy short visit meant, or know
What thy errand here below?
Shall we say that Nature blind
Check'd her hand, and changed her mind,
Just when she had exactly wrought
A finish'd pattern without fault?
Could she flag, or could she tire,
Or lack'd she the Promethean fire
(With her nine moons' long workings sicken'd)
That should thy little limbs have quicken'd?
Limbs so firm, they seem'd to assure
Life of health, and days mature:
Woman's self in miniature!
Limbs so fair, they might supply
(Themselves now but cold imagery)
The sculptor to make Beauty by.
Or did the stern-eyed Fate descry
That babe or mother, one must die;
So in mercy left the stock
And cut the branch; to save the shock

Of young years widow'd, and the pain
When single state comes back again
To the lone man who, reft of wife,
Thenceforward drags a maimèd life?
The economy of Heaven is dark,
And wisest clerks have miss'd the mark,
Why human buds, like this, should fall,
More brief than fly ephemeral
That has his day; while shrivell'd crones
Stiffen with age to stocks and stones;
And crabbèd use the conscience sears
In sinners of an hundred years.
  Mother's prattle, mother's kiss,
Baby fond, thou ne'er wilt miss:
Rites, which custom does impose,
Silver bells, and baby clothes;
Coral redder than those lips
Which pale death did late eclipse;
Music framed for infants' glee,
Whistle never tuned for thee;
Though thou want'st not, thou shalt have them,
Loving hearts were they which gave them.
Let not one be missing; nurse,
See them laid upon the hearse
Of infant slain by doom perverse.
Why should kings and nobles have
Pictured trophies to their grave,
And we, churls, to thee deny
Thy pretty toys with thee to lie—
A more harmless vanity?

CHARLES LAMB

E F B

## DEATH STANDS ABOVE ME

Death stands above me, whispering low
I know not what into my ear:
Of his strange language all I know
Is, there is not a word of fear.

WALTER SAVAGE LANDOR

## BELIEVE ME, IF ALL THOSE ENDEARING YOUNG CHARMS

Believe me, if all those endearing young charms,
Which I gaze on so fondly today,
Were to change by tomorrow, and fleet in my arms,
Like fairy-gifts fading away,
Thou wouldst still be adored, as this moment thou art,
Let thy loveliness fade as it will,
And around the dear ruin each wish of my heart
Would entwine itself verdantly still.

It is not while beauty and youth are thine own,
And thy cheeks unprofaned by a tear
That the fervor and faith of a soul can be known,
To which time will but make thee more dear;
No, the heart that has truly loved never forgets,
But as truly loves on to the close,
As the sunflower turns on her god, when he sets,
The same look which she turned when he rose.

THOMAS MOORE

## JENNY KISS'D ME

Jenny kiss'd me when we met,
Jumping from the chair she sat in;
Time, you thief, who love to get
Sweets into your list, put that in!
Say I'm weary, say I'm sad,
Say that health and wealth have miss'd me,
Say I'm growing old, but add,
Jenny kiss'd me.

LEIGH HUNT

## ABOU BEN ADHEM

Abou Ben Adhem (may his tribe increase!)
Awoke one night from a deep dream of peace,
And saw, within the moonlight in his room,
Making it rich, and like a lily in bloom,
An angel writing in a book of gold:—
Exceeding peace had made Ben Adhem bold,
And to the presence in the room he said,
"What writest thou?"—The vision rais'd its head,
And with a look made of all sweet accord,
Answer'd, "The names of those who love the Lord."
"And is mine one?" said Abou. "Nay, not so,"
Replied the angel. Abou spoke more low,
But cheerly still; and said, "I pray thee, then,
Write me as one that loves his fellow men."
The angel wrote, and vanish'd. The next night
It came again with a great wakening light,
And show'd the names whom love of God had blest,
And lo! Ben Adhem's name led all the rest.

LEIGH HUNT

## THE DESTRUCTION OF SENNACHERIB

The Assyrian came down like the wolf on the fold,
And his cohorts were gleaming in purple and gold;
And the sheen of their spears was like stars on the sea,
When the blue wave rolls nightly on deep Galilee.

Like the leaves of the forest when Summer is green,
That host with their banners at sunset were seen:
Like the leaves of the forest when Autumn hath blown,
That host on the morrow lay withered and strown.

For the Angel of Death spread his wings on the blast,
And breathed in the face of the foe as he passed;
And the eyes of the sleepers waxed deadly and chill,
And their hearts but once heaved, and for ever grew still!

And there lay the steed with his nostril all wide,
But through it there rolled not the breath of his pride:
And the foam of his gasping lay white on the turf,
And cold as the spray of the rock-beating surf.

And there lay the rider distorted and pale,
With the dew on his brow, and the rust on his mail;
And the tents were all silent, the banners alone,
The lances unlifted, the trumpet unblown.

And the widows of Ashur are loud in their wail,
And the idols are broke in the temple of Baal;
And the might of the Gentile, unsmote by the sword,
Hath melted like snow in the glance of the Lord!

George Gordon, Lord Byron

EFB

## SHE WALKS IN BEAUTY

She walks in beauty, like the night
Of cloudless climes and starry skies,
And all that's best of dark and bright
Meet in her aspect and her eyes;
Thus mellowed to that tender light
Which heaven to gaudy day denies.

One shade the more, one ray the less,
Had half impaired the nameless grace
Which waves in every raven tress
Or softly lightens o'er her face,
Where thoughts serenely sweet express
How pure, how dear their dwelling-place.

And on that cheek and o'er that brow
So soft, so calm, yet eloquent,
The smiles that win, the tints that glow
But tell of days in goodness spent,
A mind at peace with all below,
A heart whose love is innocent.

George Gordon, Lord Byron

## WE'LL GO NO MORE A-ROVING

So, we'll go no more a-roving
So late into the night,
Though the heart be still as loving,
And the moon be still as bright.

For the sword outwears its sheath,
And the soul wears out the breast,
And the heart must pause to breathe,
And love itself have rest.

Though the night was made for loving,
And the day returns too soon,
Yet we'll go no more a-roving
By the light of the moon.

George Gordon, Lord Byron

## FAREWELL

Farewell! if ever fondest prayer
For other's weal availed on high,
Mine will not all be lost in air,
But waft thy name beyond the sky.
'Twere vain to speak, to weep, to sigh:
Oh! more than tears of blood can tell,
When wrung from guilt's expiring eye,
Are in that word—Farewell!—Farewell!

These lips are mute, these eyes are dry;
But in my breast and in my brain,
Awake the pangs that pass not by,
The thought that ne'er shall sleep again.
My soul nor deigns nor dares complain,
Though grief and passion there rebel:
I only know we loved in vain;
I only feel—Farewell!—Farewell!

George Gordon, Lord Byron

# WHEN WE TWO PARTED

When we two parted
  In silence and tears,
Half broken-hearted
  To sever for years,
Pale grew thy cheek and cold,
  Colder thy kiss;
Truly that hour foretold
  Sorrow to this.

The dew of the morning
  Sunk chill on my brow—
It felt like the warning
  Of what I feel now.
Thy vows are all broken,
  And light is thy fame;
I hear thy name spoken,
  And share in its shame.

They name thee before me,
  A knell to mine ear;
A shudder comes o'er me—
  Why wert thou so dear?
They know not I knew thee,
  Who knew thee too well:—
Long, long shall I rue thee,
  Too deeply to tell.

In secret we met—
  In silence I grieve
That thy heart could forget,
  Thy spirit deceive.
If I should meet thee
  After long years,
How should I greet thee?—
  With silence and tears.

GEORGE GORDON, LORD BYRON

## TO NIGHT

Swiftly walk o'er the western wave,
    Spirit of Night!
Out of the misty eastern cave,
Where, all the long and lone daylight,
Thou wovest dreams of joy and fear,
Which make thee terrible and dear—
    Swift be thy flight!

Wrap thy form in a mantle gray,
    Star-inwrought!
Blind with thine hair the eyes of day;
Kiss her until she be wearied out,
Then wander o'er city, and sea, and land,
Touching all with thine opiate wand—
    Come, long-sought!

When I arose and saw the dawn,
    I sighed for thee;
When light rode high, and the dew was gone,
And noon lay heavy on flower and tree,
And the weary day turned to his rest,
Lingering like an unloved guest,
    I sighed for thee.

Thy brother Death came, and cried,
    Wouldst thou me?
Thy sweet child Sleep, the filmy-eyed,
Murmured like a noontide bee,
Shall I nestle near thy side?
Wouldst thou me?—And I replied,
    No, not thee!

Death will come when thou art dead,
    Soon, too soon—
Sleep will come when thou art fled;
Of neither would I ask the boon
I ask of thee, beloved Night—
Swift be thine approaching flight,
    Come soon, soon!

PERCY BYSSHE SHELLEY

## LOVE'S PHILOSOPHY

The fountains mingle with the river,
  And the rivers with the ocean,
The winds of heaven mix forever
  With a sweet emotion;
Nothing in the world is single;
  All things by a law divine
In one another's being mingle;—
  Why not I with thine?

See the mountains kiss high heaven,
  And the waves clasp one another;
No sister flower would be forgiven
  If it disdained its brother;
And the sunlight clasps the earth,
  And the moonbeams kiss the sea;
What are all these kissings worth,
  If thou kiss not me?

PERCY BYSSHE SHELLEY

## MUSIC

Music, when soft voices die,
Vibrates in the memory—
Odors, when sweet violets sicken,
Live within the sense they quicken.

Rose leaves, when the rose is dead,
Are heaped for the beloved's bed;
And so thy thoughts, when thou art gone,
Love itself shall slumber on.

PERCY BYSSHE SHELLEY

## OZYMANDIAS

I met a traveler from an antique land,
Who said: Two vast and trunkless legs of stone
Stand in the desert. Near them, on the sand,
Half sunk, a shattered visage lies, whose frown,
And wrinkled lip, and sneer of cold command,
Tell that its sculptor well those passions read,
Which yet survive, stamped on these lifeless things,
The hand that mocked them, and the heart that fed:
And on the pedestal these words appear:
"My name is Ozymandias, King of Kings:
Look on my works, ye Mighty, and despair!"
Nothing beside remains. Round the decay
Of that colossal wreck, boundless and bare
The lone and level sands stretch far away.

PERCY BYSSHE SHELLEY

## I AM

I am: yet what I am none cares or knows
  My friends forsake me like a memory lost,
I am the self-consumer of my woes—
  They rise and vanish in oblivious host,
Like shadows in love's frenzied, stifled throes—
And yet I am, and live—like vapors tossed

Into the nothingness of scorn and noise,
  Into the living sea of waking dreams,
Where there is neither sense of life or joys,
  But the vast shipwreck of my life's esteems;
Even the dearest, that I love the best,
Are strange—nay, rather stranger than the rest.

I long for scenes, where man hath never trod,
  A place where woman never smiled or wept—
There to abide with my Creator, God,
  And sleep as I in childhood sweetly slept,
Untroubling, and untroubled where I lie,
The grass below—above the vaulted sky.

John Clare

## THANATOPSIS

To him who in the love of nature holds
Communion with her visible forms, she speaks
A various language; for his gayer hours
She has a voice of gladness, and a smile
And eloquence of beauty; and she glides
Into his darker musings, with a mild
And healing sympathy that steals away
Their sharpness ere he is aware. When thoughts
Of the last bitter hour come like a blight
Over thy spirit, and sad images
Of the stern agony, and shroud, and pall,
And breathless darkness, and the narrow house,
Make thee to shudder, and grow sick at heart;—
Go forth, under the open sky, and list
To Nature's teachings, while from all around—
Earth and her waters, and the depths of air—
Comes a still voice. Yet a few days, and thee
The all-beholding sun shall see no more
In all his course; nor yet in the cold ground,
Where thy pale form was laid, with many tears,
Nor in the embrace of ocean, shall exist
Thy image. Earth, that nourished thee, shall claim
Thy growth, to be resolved to earth again,
And, lost each human trace, surrendering up
Thine individual being, shalt thou go
To mix forever with the elements,
To be a brother to the insensible rock
And to the sluggish clod, which the rude swain
Turns with his share, and treads upon. The oak
Shall send his roots abroad, and pierce thy mold.

Yet not to thine eternal resting-place
Shalt thou retire alone, nor couldst thou wish
Couch more magnificent. Thou shalt lie down
With patriarchs of the infant world—with kings,
The powerful of the earth—the wise, the good,
Fair forms, and hoary seers of ages past,
All in one mighty sepulchre. The hills
Rock-ribbed and ancient as the sun,—the vales
Stretching in pensive quietness between;
The venerable woods—rivers that move
In majesty, and the complaining brooks
That make the meadows green; and, poured round all,
Old Ocean's gray and melancholy waste,—
Are but the solemn decorations all
Of the great tomb of man. The golden sun,
The planets, all the infinite host of heaven,
Are shining on the sad abodes of death
Through the still lapse of ages. All that tread
The globe are but a handful to the tribes
That slumber in its bosom.—Take the wings
Of morning, pierce the Barcan wilderness,
Or lose thyself in the continuous woods
Where rolls the Oregon, and hears no sound,
Save his own dashings—yet the dead are there:
And millions in those solitudes, since first
The flight of years began, have laid them down
In their last sleep—the dead reign there alone.

So shalt thou rest—and what if thou withdraw
In silence from the living, and no friend
Take note of thy departure? All that breathe
Will share thy destiny. The gay will laugh
When thou art gone, the solemn brood of care
Plod on, and each one as before will chase
His favorite phantom; yet all these shall leave
Their mirth and their employments, and shall come
And make their bed with thee. As the long train
Of ages glides away, the sons of men—
The youth in life's fresh spring, and he who goes
In the full strength of years, matron and maid,
The speechless babe, and the gray-headed man—
Shall one by one be gathered to thy side,
By those, who in their turn shall follow them.

So live, that when thy summons comes to join
The innumerable caravan, which moves
To that mysterious realm, where each shall take
His chamber in the silent halls of death,
Thou go not, like the quarry-slave at night,
Scourged to his dungeon, but, sustained and soothed
By an unfaltering trust, approach thy grave
Like one who wraps the drapery of his couch
About him, and lies down to pleasant dreams.

William Cullen Bryant

## THE CHILD'S FIRST GRIEF

Oh, call my brother back to me,
I cannot play alone;
The Summer comes, with flower and bee,
Where is my brother gone?

The flowers run wild, the flowers we sowed,
Around our garden tree;
Our vine is dropping with its load—
Oh, call him back to me.

*

He wouldn't hear thy voice, fair child,
He may not come to thee;
His face that once like summer smiled,
On earth no more thou'lt see.

A rose's brief, bright life of joy,
Such unto him was given.
Go, thou must play alone, my boy,
Thy brother is in Heaven.

*

And has he left his birds and flowers?
And must I call in vain?
And through the long, long summer hours
Will he not come again?

And by the brook, and in the glade,
Are all our wanderings o'er?
Oh, while my brother with me played,
Would I have loved him more.

Felicia D. Hemans

## IT IS NOT BEAUTY I DEMAND

It is not Beauty I demand,
  A crystal brow, the moon's despair,
Nor the snow's daughter, a white hand,
  Nor mermaid's yellow pride of hair.

Tell me not of your starry eyes,
  Your lips that seem on roses fed,
Your breasts where Cupid trembling lies,
  Nor sleeps for kissing of his bed.

A bloomy pair of vermeil cheeks,
  Like Hebe's in her ruddiest hours,
A breath that softer music speaks
  Than summer winds a-wooing flowers.

These are but gauds; nay, what are lips?
  Coral beneath the ocean-stream,
Whose brink when your adventurer sips
  Full oft he perisheth on them.

And what are cheeks but ensigns oft
  That wave hot youth to fields of blood?
Did Helen's breast though ne'er so soft,
  Do Greece or Ilium any good?

Eyes can with baleful ardor burn,
  Poison can breath that erst perfumed,
There's many a white hand holds an urn
  With lovers' hearts to dust consumed.

For crystal brows—there's naught within,
  They are but empty cells for pride;
He who the Syren's hair would win
  Is mostly strangled in the tide.

Give me, instead of beauty's bust,
  A tender heart, a loyal mind,
Which with temptation I could trust,
  Yet never linked with error find.

One in whose gentle bosom I
  Could pour my secret heart of woes,
Like the care-burdened honey-fly
  That hides his murmurs in the rose.

George Darley

## ON THE GRASSHOPPER AND CRICKET

The poetry of earth is never dead:
  When all the birds are faint with the hot sun,
  And hide in cooling trees, a voice will run
From hedge to hedge about the new-mown mead;
That is the grasshopper's—he takes the lead
  In summer luxury,—he has never done
  With his delights, for when tired out with fun
He rests at ease beneath some pleasant weed.
The poetry of earth is ceasing never:
  On a lone winter evening, when the frost
Has wrought a silence, from the stove there shrills
The cricket's song, in warmth increasing ever,
  And seems to one, in drowsiness half-lost,
The grasshopper's among some grassy hills.

John Keats

CFB

## LA BELLE DAME SANS MERCI

"O what can ail thee, knight-at-arms,
  Alone and palely loitering?
The sedge has wither'd from the lake,
        And no birds sing.

"O what can ail thee, knight-at-arms,
  So haggard and so woe-begone?
The squirrel's granary is full,
        And the harvest's done.

"I see a lily on thy brow
  With anguish moist and fever dew;
And on thy cheek a fading rose
        Fast withereth too."

"I met a lady in the meads,
  Full beautiful—a faery's child,
Her hair was long, her foot was light,
        And her eyes were wild.

"I made a garland for her head,
  And bracelets too, and fragrant zone;
She look'd at me as she did love,
        And made sweet moan.

"I set her on my pacing steed
  And nothing else saw all day long,
For sideways would she lean, and sing
        A faery's song.

"She found me roots of relish sweet,
And honey wild and manna dew,
And sure in language strange she said,
"I love thee true!"

"She took me to her elfin grot,
And there she wept and sigh'd full sore;
And there I shut her wild, wild eyes
With kisses four.

"And there she lullèd me asleep,
And there I dream'd—Ah! woe betide!
The latest dream I ever dream'd
On the cold hill side.

"I saw pale kings and princes too,
Pale warriors, death-pale were they all;
Who cried—"La Belle Dame sans Merci
Hath thee in thrall!"

"I saw their starved lips in the gloam
With horrid warning gapèd wide,
And I awoke and found me here
On the cold hill's side.

"And this is why I sojourn here
Alone and palely loitering,
Though the sedge has wither'd from the lake,
And no birds sing."

John Keats

## ODE TO A NIGHTINGALE

My heart aches, and a drowsy numbness pains
My sense, as though of hemlock I had drunk,
Or emptied some dull opiate to the drains
One minute past, and Lethe-wards had sunk:
'Tis not through envy of thy happy lot,
But being too happy in thy happiness,—
That thou, light-winged Dryad of the trees,
In some melodious plot
Of beechen green, and shadows numberless,
Singest of summer in full-throated ease.

O for a draught of vintage, that hath been
Cooled a long age in the deep-delved earth,
Tasting of Flora and the country green,
Dance, and Provençal song, and sun-burnt mirth!
O for a beaker full of the warm South,
Full of the true, the blushful Hippocrene,
With beaded bubbles winking at the brim,
And purple-stained mouth;
That I might drink, and leave the world unseen,
And with thee fade away into the forest dim:

Fade far away, dissolve, and quite forget
What thou among the leaves hast never known,
The weariness, the fever, and the fret
Here, where men sit and hear each other groan;
Where palsy shakes a few, sad, last gray hairs,
Where youth grows pale, and spectre-thin, and dies;
Where but to think is to be full of sorrow
And leaden-eyed despairs;
Where beauty cannot keep her lustrous eyes,
Or new love pine at them beyond tomorrow.

Away! away! for I will fly to thee,
   Not charioted by Bacchus and his pards,
But on the viewless wings of Poesy,
   Though the dull brain perplexes and retards:
Already with thee! tender is the night,
   And haply the Queen-Moon is on her throne,
      Clustered around by all her starry fays;
            But here there is no light,
   Save what from heaven is with the breezes blown
      Through verdurous glooms and winding mossy ways.

I cannot see what flowers are at my feet,
   Nor what soft incense hangs upon the boughs,
But, in embalmed darkness, guess each sweet
   Wherewith the seasonable month endows
The grass, the thicket, and the fruit-tree wild;
   White hawthorn, and the pastoral eglantine;
      Fast-fading violets covered up in leaves;
            And mid-May's eldest child,
   The coming musk-rose, full of dewy wine,
      The murmurous haunt of flies on summer eves.

Darkling I listen; and for many a time
   I have been half in love with easeful Death,
Called him soft names in many a mused rhyme,
   To take into the air my quiet breath;
Now more than ever seems it rich to die,
   To cease upon the midnight with no pain,
      While thou art pouring forth thy soul abroad
            In such an ecstasy!
   Still wouldst thou sing, and I have ears in vain—
      To thy high requiem become a sod.

Thou wast not born for death, immortal Bird!
  No hungry generations tread thee down;
The voice I hear this passing night was heard
  In ancient days by emperor and clown:
Perhaps the self-same song that found a path
  Through the sad heart of Ruth, when, sick for home,
    She stood in tears amid the alien corn;
        The same that oft-times hath
  Charmed magic casements, opening on the foam
    Of perilous seas, in faery lands forlorn.

Forlorn! the very word is like a bell
  To toll me back from thee to my sole self!
Adieu! the fancy cannot cheat so well
  As she is famed to do, deceiving elf.
Adieu! adieu! thy plaintive anthem fades
  Past the near meadows, over the still stream,
    Up the hill-side; and now 'tis buried deep
        In the next valley-glades:
  Was it a vision, or a waking dream?
    Fled is that music:—do I wake or sleep?

John Keats

## ODE ON A GRECIAN URN

Thou still unravish'd bride of quietness,
Thou foster-child of silence and slow time,
Sylvan historian, who canst thus express
A flowery tale more sweetly than our rhyme:
What leaf-fring'd legend haunts about thy shape
Of deities or mortals, or of both,
In Tempe or the dales of Arcady?
What men or gods are these? What maidens loth?
What mad pursuit? What struggle to escape?
What pipes and timbrels? What wild ecstasy?

Heard melodies are sweet, but those unheard
Are sweeter; therefore, ye soft pipes, play on;
Not to the sensual ear, but more endear'd,
Pipe to the spirit ditties of no tone:
Fair youth, beneath the trees, thou canst not leave
Thy song, nor ever can those trees be bare;
Bold Lover, never, never canst thou kiss,
Though winning near the goal—yet, do not grieve;
She cannot fade, though thou hast not thy bliss,
For ever wilt thou love, and she be fair!

Ah, happy, happy boughs! that cannot shed
Your leaves, nor ever bid the Spring adieu;
And, happy melodist, unwearièd,
For ever piping songs for ever new;
More happy love! more happy, happy love!
For ever warm and still to be enjoy'd,
For ever panting, and for ever young;
All breathing human passion far above,
That leaves a heart high-sorrowful and cloy'd,
A burning forehead, and a parching tongue.

Who are these coming to the sacrifice?
To what green altar, O mysterious priest,
Lead'st thou that heifer lowing at the skies,
And all her silken flanks with garlands drest?
What little town by river or sea shore,
Or mountain-built with peaceful citadel,
Is emptied of this folk, this pious morn?
And, little town, thy streets for evermore
Will silent be; and not a soul to tell
Why thou art desolate, can e'er return.

O Attic shape! Fair attitude! with brede
Of marble men and maidens overwrought,
With forest branches and the trodden weed;
Thou, silent form, dost tease us out of thought
As doth eternity. Cold Pastoral!
When old age shall this generation waste,
Thou shalt remain, in midst of other woe
Than ours, a friend to man, to whom thou say'st,
"Beauty is truth, truth beauty—that is all
Ye know on earth, and all ye need to know."

JOHN KEATS

## I REMEMBER, I REMEMBER

I remember, I remember
The house where I was born,
The little window where the sun
Came peeping in at morn;
He never came a wink too soon
Nor brought too long a day;
But now, I often wish the night
Had borne my breath away.

I remember, I remember
The roses, red and white,
The violets, and the lily-cups—
Those flowers made of light!
The lilacs where the robin built,
And where my brother set
The laburnum on his birthday,—
The tree is living yet!

I remember, I remember
Where I used to swing,
And thought the air must rush as fresh
To swallows on the wing;
My spirit flew in feathers then
That is so heavy now,
The summer pools could hardly cool
The fever on my brow.

I remember, I remember
The fir trees dark and high;
I used to think their slender tops
Were close against the sky:
It was a childish ignorance,
But now 'tis little joy
To know I'm farther off from Heaven
Than when I was a boy.

THOMAS HOOD

## CONCORD HYMN

By the rude bridge that arched the flood,
Their flag to April's breeze unfurled,
Here once the embattled farmers stood,
And fired the shot heard round the world.

The foe long since in silence slept;
Alike the conqueror silent sleeps;
And Time the ruined bridge has swept
Down the dark stream that seaward creeps.

On this green bank, by this soft stream,
We set today a votive stone;
That memory may their deed redeem,
When, like our sires, our sons are gone.

Spirit, that made those heroes dare
To die, and leave their children free,
Bid Time and Nature gently spare
The shaft we raise to them and thee.

RALPH WALDO EMERSON

## SONNETS FROM THE PORTUGUESE

### 6

Go from me. Yet I feel that I shall stand
Henceforward in thy shadow. Nevermore
Alone upon the threshold of my door
Of individual life, I shall command
The uses of my soul, nor lift my hand
Serenely in the sunshine as before,
Without the sense of that which I forbore—
Thy touch upon the palm. The widest land
Doom takes to part us, leaves thy heart in mine
With pulses that beat double. What I do
And what I dream include thee, as the wine
Must taste of its own grapes. And when I sue
God for myself, He hears that name of thine,
And sees within my eyes the tears of two.

### 16

If thou must love me, let it be for naught
Except for love's sake only. Do not say,
"I love her for her smile—her look—her way
Of speaking gently—for a trick of thought
That falls in well with mine, and certes brought
A sense of pleasant ease on such a day"—
For these things in themselves, Belovèd, may
Be changed, or change for thee—and love, so wrought,
May be unwrought so. Neither love me for
Thine own dear pity's wiping my cheeks dry—
A creature might forget to weep, who bore
Thy comfort long, and lose thy love thereby!
But love me for love's sake, that evermore
Thou may'st love on, through love's eternity.

32

The first time that the sun rose on thine oath
To love me, I looked forward to the moon
To slacken all those bonds which seemed too soon
And quickly tied to make a lasting troth.
Quick-loving hearts, I thought, may quickly loathe;
And, looking on myself, I seemed not one
For such man's love!—more like an out-of-tune
Worn viol, a good singer would be wroth
To spoil his song with, and which, snatched in haste,
Is laid down at the first ill-sounding note.
I did not wrong myself so, but I placed
A wrong on *thee*. For perfect strains may float
'Neath master-hands, from instruments defaced—
And great souls, at one stroke, may do and dote.

43

How do I love thee? Let me count the ways.
I love thee to the depth and breadth and height
My soul can reach, when feeling out of sight
For the ends of Being and ideal Grace.
I love thee to the level of every day's
Most quiet need, by sun and candle-light.
I love thee freely, as men strive for right;
I love thee purely, as they turn from praise.
I love thee with the passion put to use
In my old griefs, and with my childhood's faith.
I love thee with a love I seemed to lose
With my lost saints—I love thee with the breath,
Smiles, tears, of all my life—and, if God choose,
I shall but love thee better after death.

ELIZABETH BARRETT BROWNING

## THE CHILDREN'S HOUR

Between the dark and the daylight,
  When the night is beginning to lower,
Comes a pause in the day's occupations,
  That is known as the children's hour.

I hear in the chamber above me
  The patter of little feet,
The sound of a door that is opened,
  And voices soft and sweet.

From my study I see in the lamplight,
  Descending the broad hall stair,
Grave Alice, and laughing Allegra,
  And Edith with golden hair.

A whisper, and then a silence:
  Yet I know by their merry eyes
They are plotting and planning together
  To take me by surprise.

A sudden rush from the stairway,
  A sudden raid from the hall!
By three doors left unguarded
  They enter my castle wall!

They climb up into my turret
  O'er the arms and back of my chair;
If I try to escape, they surround me;
  They seem to be everywhere.

They almost devour me with kisses,
  Their arms about me entwine,
Till I think of the Bishop of Bingen
  In his Mouse-Tower on the Rhine!

Do you think, O blue-eyed banditti,
  Because you have scaled the wall,
Such an old mustache as I am
  Is not a match for you all!

I have you fast in my fortress,
  And will not let you depart,
But put you down into the dungeon
  In the round-tower of my heart.

And there will I keep you forever,
  Yes, forever and a day.
Till the walls shall crumble to ruin,
  And moulder in dust away!

HENRY WADSWORTH LONGFELLOW

## PAUL REVERE'S RIDE

Listen, my children, and you shall hear
Of the midnight ride of Paul Revere,
On the eighteenth of April, in Seventy-five;
Hardly a man is now alive
Who remembers that famous day and year.

He said to his friend, "If the British march
By land or sea from the town tonight,
Hang a lantern aloft in the belfry arch
Of the North Church tower as a signal light—
One, if by land, and two, if by sea;
And I on the opposite shore will be,
Ready to ride and spread the alarm
Through every Middlesex village and farm,
For the country folk to be up and to arm."

Then he said, "Good night!" and with muffled oar
Silently rowed to the Charlestown shore,
Just as the moon rose over the bay,
Where swinging wide at her moorings lay
The Somerset, British man-of-war;
A phantom ship, with each mast and spar
Across the moon like a prison bar,
And a huge black hulk, that was magnified
By its own reflection in the tide.

Meanwhile, his friend, through alley and street,
Wanders and watches with eager ears,
Till in the silence around him he hears
The muster of men at the barrack door,
The sound of arms, and the tramp of feet,
And the measured tread of the grenadiers,
Marching down to their boats on the shore.

Then he climbed the tower of the Old North Church,
By the wooden stairs, with stealthy tread,
To the belfry-chamber overhead,
And startled the pigeons from their perch
On the somber rafters, that round him made
Masses and moving shapes of shade—
By the trembling ladder, steep and tall,
To the highest window in the wall,
Where he paused to listen and look down
A moment on the roofs of the town,
And the moonlight flowing over all.

Beneath, in the churchyard, lay the dead,
In their night-encampment on the hill,
Wrapped in silence so deep and still
That he could hear, like a sentinel's tread,
The watchful night-wind, as it went
Creeping along from tent to tent,
And seeming to whisper, "All is well!"
A moment only he feels the spell
Of the place and the hour, and the secret dread
Of the lonely belfry and the dead;
For suddenly all his thoughts are bent
On a shadowy something far away,
Where the river widens to meet the bay—
A line of black that bends and floats
On the rising tide, like a bridge of boats.

Meanwhile, impatient to mount and ride,
Booted and spurred, with a heavy stride
On the opposite shore walked Paul Revere.
Now he patted his horse's side,
Now gazed at the landscape far and near,
Then, impetuous, stamped the earth,
And turned and tightened his saddle-girth;
But mostly he watched with eager search
The belfry-tower of the Old North Church,
As it rose above the graves on the hill,

Lonely and spectral and somber and still.
And lo! as he looks, on the belfry's height
A glimmer, and then a gleam of light!
He springs to the saddle, the bridle he turns,
But lingers and gazes, till full on his sight
A second lamp in the belfry burns!

A hurry of hoofs in a village street,
A shape in the moonlight, a bulk in the dark,
And beneath, from the pebbles, in passing, a spark
Struck out by a steed flying fearless and fleet;
That was all! And yet, through the gloom and the light,
The fate of a nation was riding that night;
And the spark struck out by that steed in his flight,
Kindled the land into flame with its heat.

He has left the village and mounted the steep,
And beneath him, tranquil and broad and deep,
Is the Mystic, meeting the ocean tides;
And under the alders that skirt its edge,
Now soft on the sand, now loud on the ledge,
Is heard the tramp of his steed as he rides.

It was twelve by the village clock,
When he crossed the bridge into Medford town.
He heard the crowing of the cock,
And the barking of the farmer's dog,
And felt the damp of the river fog,
That rises after the sun goes down.

It was one by the village clock,
When he galloped into Lexington.
He saw the gilded weathercock
Swim in the moonlight as he passed,
And the meeting-house windows, blank and bare,
Gaze at him with a spectral glare,
As if they already stood aghast
At the bloody work they would look upon.

It was two by the village clock,
When he came to the bridge in Concord town.
He heard the bleating of the flock,
And the twitter of birds among the trees,
And felt the breath of the morning breeze
Blowing over the meadows brown.
And one was safe and asleep in his bed
Who at the bridge would be first to fall,
Who that day would be lying dead,
Pierced by a British musket-ball.

You know the rest. In the books you have read,
How the British Regulars fired and fled—
How the farmers gave them ball for ball,
From behind each fence and farmyard wall,
Chasing the redcoats down the lane,
Then crossing the fields to emerge again
Under the trees at the turn of the road,
And only pausing to fire and load.
So through the night rode Paul Revere;
And so through the night went his cry of alarm
To every Middlesex village and farm—
A cry of defiance, and not of fear,
A voice in the darkness, a knock at the door,
And a word that shall echo forevermore!
For, borne on the night-wind of the Past,
Through all our history, to the last,
In the hour of darkness and peril and need,
The people will waken and listen to hear
The hurrying hoofbeats of that steed,
And the midnight message of Paul Revere.

Henry Wadsworth Longfellow

## THE DAY IS DONE

The day is done, and the darkness
  Falls from the wings of Night,
As a feather is wafted downward
  From an eagle in his flight.

I see the lights of the village
  Gleam through the rain and the mist,
And a feeling of sadness comes o'er me
  That my soul cannot resist:

A feeling of sadness and longing,
  That is not akin to pain,
And resembles sorrow only
  As the mist resembles the rain.

Come, read to me some poem,
  Some simple and heartfelt lay,
That shall soothe this restless feeling,
  And banish the thoughts of day.

Not from the grand old masters,
  Not from the bards sublime,
Whose distant footsteps echo
  Through the corridors of Time,

For, like strains of martial music,
  Their mighty thoughts suggest
Life's endless toil and endeavor;
  And tonight I long for rest.

Read from some humbler poet,
  Whose songs gushed from his heart,
As showers from the clouds of summer,
  Or tears from the eyelids start;

Who, through long days of labor,
  And nights devoid of ease,
Still heard in his soul the music
  Of wonderful melodies.

Such songs have power to quiet
  The restless pulse of care,
And come like the benediction
  That follows after prayer.

Then read from the treasured volume
  The poem of thy choice,
And lend to the rhyme of the poet
  The beauty of thy voice.

And the night shall be filled with music,
  And the cares, that infest the day,
Shall fold their tents, like the Arabs,
  And as silently steal away.

HENRY WADSWORTH LONGFELLOW

## THE BAREFOOT BOY

Blessings on thee, little man,
Barefoot boy, with cheek of tan!
With thy turned-up pantaloons,
And thy merry whistled tunes;
With thy red lip, redder still
Kissed by strawberries on the hill;
With the sunshine on thy face,
Through thy torn brim's jaunty grace;
From my heart I give thee joy,—
I was once a barefoot boy!
Prince thou art,—the grown-up man
Only is republican.
Let the million-dollared ride!
Barefoot, trudging at his side,
Thou hast more than he can buy
In the reach of ear and eye,—
Outward sunshine, inward joy:
Blessings on thee, barefoot boy!

O for boyhood's painless play,
Sleep that wakes in laughing day,
Health that mocks the doctor's rules,
Knowledge never learned of schools,
Of the wild bee's morning chase,
Of the wild-flower's time and place,
Flight of fowl and habitude
Of the tenants of the wood;
How the tortoise bears his shell,
How the woodchuck digs his cell,
And the ground-mole sinks his well;
How the robin feeds her young,
How the oriole's nest is hung;
Where the whitest lilies blow,
Where the freshest berries grow,

Where the ground-nut trails its vine,
Where the wood-grape's clusters shine;
Of the black wasp's cunning way,
Mason of his walls of clay,
And the architectural plans
Of gray hornet artisans!—
For, eschewing books and tasks,
Nature answers all he asks;
Hand in hand with her he walks,
Face to face with her he talks,
Part and parcel of her joy—
Blessings on the barefoot boy!

O for boyhood's time of June,
Crowding years in one brief moon,
When all things I heard or saw,
Me, their master, waited for.
I was rich in flowers and trees,
Humming-birds and honey-bees;
For my sport the squirrel played,
Plied the snouted mole his spade;
For my taste the blackberry cone
Purpled over hedge and stone;
Laughed the brook for my delight
Through the day and through the night,
Whispering at the garden wall,
Talked with me from fall to fall;
Mine the sand-rimmed pickerel pond,
Mine the walnut slopes beyond,
Mine, on bending orchard trees,
Apples of Hesperides!
Still as my horizon grew,
Larger grew my riches too;
All the world I saw or knew
Seemed a complex Chinese toy,
Fashioned for a barefoot boy!

O for festal dainties spread,
Like my bowl of milk and bread,—
Pewter spoon and bowl of wood,
On the door-stone, gray and rude!
O'er me, like a regal tent,
Cloudy-ribbed, the sunset bent,
Purple-curtained, fringed with gold,
Looped in many a wind-swung fold;
While for music came the play
Of the pied frogs' orchestra;
And, to light the noisy choir,
Lit the fly his lamp of fire.
I was monarch: pomp and joy
Waited on the barefoot boy!

Cheerily, then, my little man,
Live and laugh, as boyhood can!
Though the flinty slopes be hard,
Stubble-speared the new-mown sward,
Every morn shall lead thee through
Fresh baptisms of the dew;
Every evening from thy feet
Shall the cool wind kiss the heat:
All too soon these feet must hide
In the prison cells of pride,
Lose the freedom of the sod,
Like a colt's for work be shod,
Made to tread the mills of toil,
Up and down in ceaseless moil:
Happy if their track be found
Never on forbidden ground;
Happy if they sink not in
Quick and treacherous sands of sin.
Ah! that thou couldst know thy joy,
Ere it passes, barefoot boy!

JOHN GREENLEAF WHITTIER

## ANNABEL LEE

It was many and many a year ago,
In a kingdom by the sea,
That a maiden there lived whom you may know
By the name of Annabel Lee;—
And this maiden she lived with no other thought
Than to love and be loved by me.

She was a child and I was a child,
In this kingdom by the sea,
But we loved with a love that was more than love—
I and my Annabel Lee—
With a love that the winged seraphs of Heaven
Coveted her and me.

And this was the reason that, long ago,
In this kingdom by the sea,
A wind blew out of a cloud, by night
Chilling my Annabel Lee;
So that her highborn kinsmen came
And bore her away from me,
To shut her up in a sepulchre
In this kingdom by the sea.

The angels, not half so happy in Heaven,
Went envying her and me:
Yes! that was the reason (as all men know,
In this kingdom by the sea)
That the wind came out of the cloud, chilling
And killing my Annabel Lee.

But our love it was stronger by far than the love
Of those who were older than we—
Of many far wiser than we—
And neither the angels in Heaven above
Nor the demons down under the sea,
Can ever dissever my soul from the soul
Of the beautiful Annabel Lee:—

For the moon never beams without bringing me dreams
  Of the beautiful Annabel Lee;
And the stars never rise but I see the bright eyes
  Of the beautiful Annabel Lee;
And so, all the night-tide, I lie down by the side
Of my darling, my darling, my life and my bride,
  In her sepulchre there by the sea—
  In her tomb by the sounding sea.

EDGAR ALLAN POE

## THE RAVEN

Once upon a midnight dreary, while I pondered, weak and weary,
Over many a quaint and curious volume of forgotten lore,—
While I nodded, nearly napping, suddenly there came a tapping,
As of some one gently rapping, rapping at my chamber door.
" 'Tis some visitor," I muttered, "tapping at my chamber door:
  Only this and nothing more."

Ah, distinctly I remember it was in the bleak December,
And each separate dying ember wrought its ghost upon the floor.
Eagerly I wished the morrow;—vainly I had sought to borrow
From my books surcease of sorrow—sorrow for the lost Lenore,
For the rare and radiant maiden whom the angels name Lenore:
  Nameless here for evermore.

And the silken sad uncertain rustling of each purple curtain
Thrilled me—filled me with fantastic terrors never felt before;
So that now, to still the beating of my heart, I stood repeating,
" 'Tis some visitor entreating entrance at my chamber door,
Some late visitor entreating entrance at my chamber door:
This it is and nothing more."

Presently my soul grew stronger; hesitating then no longer,
"Sir," said I, "or Madam, truly your forgiveness I implore;
But the fact is I was napping, and so gently you came rapping,
And so faintly you came tapping, tapping at my chamber door,
That I scarce was sure I heard you"—here I opened wide the door:—
Darkness there and nothing more.

Deep into that darkness peering, long I stood there wondering, fearing,
Doubting, dreaming dreams no mortals ever dared to dream before;
But the silence was unbroken, and the stillness gave no token,
And the only word there spoken was the whispered word, "Lenore!"
This I whispered, and an echo murmured back the word, "Lenore!"
Merely this and nothing more.

Back into the chamber turning, all my soul within me burning,
Soon again I heard a tapping somewhat louder than before.
"Surely," said I, "surely that is something at my window lattice;

Let me see, then, what thereat is, and this mystery explore;
Let my heart be still a moment and this mystery explore;
'Tis the wind and nothing more."

Open here I flung the shutter, when, with many a flirt and flutter,
In there stepped a stately Raven of the saintly days of yore.
Not the least obeisance made he; not a minute stopped or stayed he;
But, with mien of lord or lady, perched above my chamber door,
Perched upon a bust of Pallas just above my chamber door;
Perched, and sat, and nothing more.

Then this ebony bird beguiling my sad fancy into smiling
By the grave and stern decorum of the countenance it wore,—
"Though thy crest be shorn and shaven, thou," I said, "art sure no craven,
Ghastly grim and ancient Raven wandering from the Nightly shore:
Tell me what thy lordly name is on the Night's Plutonian shore!"
Quoth the Raven, "Nevermore."

Much I marvelled this ungainly fowl to hear discourse so plainly,
Though its answer little meaning—little relevancy bore;
For we cannot help agreeing that no living human being
Ever yet was blessed with seeing bird above his chamber door,
Bird or beast upon the sculptured bust above his chamber door,
With such name as "Nevermore."

But the Raven, sitting lonely on the placid bust, spoke only
That one word, as if his soul in that one word he did outpour.
Nothing further then he uttered, not a feather then he fluttered,
Till I scarcely more than muttered,—"Other friends have flown before;
On the morrow *he* will leave me, as my Hopes have flown before."
Then the bird said, "Nevermore."

Startled at the stillness broken by reply so aptly spoken,
"Doubtless," said I, "what it utters is its only stock and store,
Caught from some unhappy master whom unmerciful Disaster
Followed fast and followed faster till his songs one burden bore:
Till the dirges of his Hope that melancholy burden bore
Of 'Never—nevermore.' "

But the Raven still beguiling all my sad soul into smiling,
Straight I wheeled a cushioned seat in front of bird and bust and door;
Then, upon the velvet sinking, I betook myself to linking
Fancy unto fancy, thinking what this ominous bird of yore,
What this grim, ungainly, ghastly, gaunt, and ominous bird of yore
Meant in croaking "Nevermore."

This I sat engaged in guessing, but no syllable expressing
To the fowl whose fiery eyes now burned into my bosom's core;
This and more I sat divining, with my head at ease reclining
On the cushion's velvet lining that the lamplight gloated o'er,
But whose velvet violet lining with the lamp-light gloating o'er
*She* shall press, ah, nevermore!

Then, methought, the air grew denser, perfumed from an
unseen censer
Swung by seraphim whose foot-falls tinkled on the tufted
floor.
"Wretch," I cried, "thy God hath lent thee—by these angels
he hath sent thee
Respite—respite and nepenthe from thy memories of
Lenore!
Quaff, oh quaff this kind nepenthe, and forget this lost
Lenore!"
Quoth the Raven, "Nevermore."

"Prophet!" said I, "thing of evil! prophet still, if bird or
devil!
Whether Tempter sent, or whether tempest tossed thee here
ashore,
Desolate, yet all undaunted, on this desert land enchanted—
On this home by Horror haunted—tell me truly, I implore:
Is there—*is* there balm in Gilead?—tell me—tell me, I
implore!"
Quoth the Raven, "Nevermore."

"Prophet!" said I, "thing of evil! prophet still, if bird or
devil!
By that Heaven that bends above us, by that God we both
adore,
Tell this soul with sorrow laden if, within the distant
Aidenn,
It shall clasp a sainted maiden whom the angels name
Lenore:
Clasp a rare and radiant maiden whom the angels name
Lenore!"
Quoth the Raven, "Nevermore."

"Be that word our sign of parting, bird or fiend!" I shrieked, upstarting;
"Get thee back into the tempest and the Night's Plutonian shore!
Leave no black plume as a token of that lie thy soul hath spoken!
Leave my loneliness unbroken! quit the bust above my door!
Take thy beak from out my heart, and take thy form from off my door!"
Quoth the Raven, "Nevermore."

And the Raven, never flitting, still is sitting, still is sitting
On the pallid bust of Pallas just above my chamber door;
And his eyes have all the seeming of a demon's that is dreaming,
And the lamp-light o'er him streaming throws his shadow on the floor;
And my soul from out that shadow that lies floating on the floor
Shall be lifted—nevermore!

Edgar Allan Poe

## THE CHAMBERED NAUTILUS

This is the ship of pearl, which, poets feign,
Sail the unshadowed main,—
The venturous bark that flings
On the sweet summer wind its purpled wings
In gulfs enchanted, where the Siren sings,
And coral reefs lie bare,
Where the cold sea-maids rise to sun their streaming hair.

Its webs of living gauze no more unfurl;
Wrecked is the ship of pearl!
And every chambered cell,
Where its dim dreaming life was wont to dwell,
As the frail tenant shaped his growing shell,
Before thee lies revealed,—
Its irised ceiling rent, its sunless crypt unsealed!

Year after year beheld the silent toil
That spread his lustrous coil;
Still, as the spiral grew,
He left the past year's dwelling for the new,
Stole with soft step its shining archway through,
Built up its idle door,
Stretched in his last-found home, and knew the old no more.

Thanks for the heavenly message brought by thee,
Child of the wandering sea,
Cast from her lap, forlorn!
From thy dead lips a clearer note is born
Than ever Triton blew from wreathéd horn!
While on mine ear it rings,
Through the deep caves of thought I hear a voice that sings:—

Build thee more stately mansions, O my soul,
As the swift seasons roll!
Leave thy low-vaulted past!
Let each new temple, nobler than the last,
Shut thee from heaven with a dome more vast,
Till thou at length art free,
Leaving thine outgrown shell by life's unresting sea!

Oliver Wendell Holmes

## BREAK, BREAK, BREAK

Break, break, break,
  On thy cold gray stones, O Sea!
And I would that my tongue could utter
  The thoughts that arise in me.

O well for the fisherman's boy,
  That he shouts with his sister at play!
O well for the sailor lad,
  That he sings in his boat on the bay!

And the stately ships go on
  To their haven under the hill;
But O for the touch of a vanished hand,
  And the sound of a voice that is still!

Break, break, break,
  At the foot of thy crags, O Sea!
But the tender grace of a day that is dead
  Will never come back to me.

ALFRED, LORD TENNYSON

## CROSSING THE BAR

Sunset and evening star,
  And one clear call for me!
And may there be no moaning of the bar,
  When I put out to sea,

But such a tide as moving seems asleep,
  Too full for sound and foam,
When that which drew from out the boundless deep
  Turns again home.

Twilight and evening bell,
  And after that the dark!
And may there be no sadness of farewell;
  When I embark;

For tho' from out our bourne of Time and Place
  The flood may bear me far,
I hope to see my Pilot face to face
  When I have crost the bar.

ALFRED, LORD TENNYSON

## RING OUT, WILD BELLS

Ring out, wild bells, to the wild sky,
The flying cloud, the frosty light:
The year is dying in the night;
Ring out, wild bells, and let him die.

Ring out the old, ring in the new,
Ring, happy bells, across the snow;
The year is going, let him go;
Ring out the false, ring in the true.

Ring out the grief that saps the mind,
For those that here we see no more;
Ring out the feud of rich and poor,
Ring in redress to all mankind.

Ring out a slowly dying cause,
And ancient forms of party strife;
Ring in the nobler modes of life,
With sweeter manners, purer laws.

Ring out the want, the care, the sin,
The faithless coldness of the times;
Ring out, ring out my mournful rhymes,
But ring the fuller minstrel in.

Ring out false pride in place and blood,
The civic slander and the spite;
Ring in the love of truth and right,
Ring in the common love of good.

Ring out old shapes of foul disease,
Ring out the narrowing lust of gold;
Ring out the thousand wars of old,
Ring in the thousand years of peace.

Ring in the valiant man and free,
The larger heart, the kindlier hand;
Ring out the darkness of the land,
Ring in the Christ that is to be.

ALFRED, LORD TENNYSON

## SWEET AND LOW

Sweet and low, sweet and low,
Wind of the western sea,
Low, low, breathe and blow,
Wind of the western sea!
Over the rolling waters go,
Come from the dying moon, and blow,
Blow him again to me;
While my little one, while my pretty one, sleeps.

Sleep and rest, sleep and rest,
Father will come to thee soon;
Rest, rest, on mother's breast,
Father will come to thee soon;
Father will come to his babe in the nest,
Silver sails all out of the west
Under the silver moon:
Sleep, my little one, sleep, my pretty one, sleep.

ALFRED, LORD TENNYSON

# MY LAST DUCHESS

SCENE: FERRARA

That's my last Duchess painted on the wall,
Looking as if she were alive. I call
That piece a wonder, now: Frà Pandolf's hands
Worked busily a day, and there she stands.
Will't please you sit and look at her? I said
"Frà Pandolf" by design, for never read
Strangers like you that pictured countenance,
The depth and passion of its earnest glance,
But to myself they turned (since none puts by
The curtain I have drawn for you, but I)
And seemed as they would ask me, if they durst,
How such a glance came there; so, not the first
Are you to turn and ask thus. Sir, 'twas not
Her husband's presence only, called that spot
Of joy into the Duchess' cheek: perhaps
Frà Pandolf chanced to say, "Her mantle laps
Over my Lady's wrist too much," or "Paint
Must never hope to reproduce the faint
Half-flush that dies along her throat"; such stuff
Was courtesy, she thought, and cause enough
For calling up that spot of joy. She had
A heart—how shall I say?—too soon made glad,
Too easily impressed; she liked whate'er
She looked on, and her looks went everywhere.
Sir, 'twas all one! My favor at her breast,
The dropping of the daylight in the West,
The bough of cherries some officious fool
Broke in the orchard for her, the white mule
She rode with round the terrace—all and each
Would draw from her alike the approving speech,
Or blush, at least. She thanked men,—good; but thanked
Somehow—I know not how—as if she ranked

My gift of a nine-hundred-years'-old name
With anybody's gift. Who'd stoop to blame
This sort of trifling? Even had you skill
In speech—(which I have not)—to make your will
Quite clear to such an one, and say, "Just this
Or that in you disgusts me; here you miss,
Or there exceed the mark"—and if she let
Herself be lessoned so, nor plainly set
Her wits to yours, forsooth, and made excuse,
—E'en then would be some stooping, and I choose
Never to stoop. Oh, sir, she smiled, no doubt,
Whene'er I passed her; but who passed without
Much the same smile? This grew; I gave commands;
Then all smiles stopped together. There she stands
As if alive. Will't please you rise? We'll meet
The company below, then. I repeat,
The Count your master's known munificence
Is ample warrant that no just pretense
Of mine for dowry will be disallowed;
Though his fair daughter's self, as I avowed
At starting, is my object. Nay, we'll go
Together down, sir! Notice Neptune, though,
Taming a sea-horse, thought a rarity,
Which Claus of Innsbruck cast in bronze for me!

Robert Browning

## PROSPICE

Fear death?—to feel the fog in my throat,
The mist in my face,
When the snows begin, and the blasts denote
I am nearing the place,
The power of the night, the press of the storm,
The post of the foe;
Where he stands, the Arch Fear in a visible form,
Yet the strong man must go:
For the journey is done and the summit attained,
And the barriers fall,
Though a battle's to fight ere the guerdon be gained,
The reward of it all.
I was ever a fighter, so—one fight more,
The best and the last!
I would hate that death bandaged my eyes, and forbore,
And bade me creep past.
No! let me taste the whole of it, fare like my peers
The heroes of old,
Bear the brunt, in a minute pay glad life's arrears
Of pain, darkness and cold.
For sudden the worse turns the best to the brave,
The black minute's at end,
And the elements' rage, the fiend-voices that rave,
Shall dwindle, shall blend,
Shall change, shall become first a peace out of pain,
Then a light, then thy breast,
O thou soul of my soul! I shall clasp thee again,
And with God be the rest!

ROBERT BROWNING

## THE OWL AND THE PUSSY-CAT

The Owl and the Pussy-cat went to sea
  In a beautiful pea-green boat:
They took some honey, and plenty of money
  Wrapped up in a five-pound note.
The Owl looked up to the stars above,
  And sang to a small guitar,
"O lovely Pussy, O Pussy, my love,
  What a beautiful Pussy you are,
      You are,
      You are!
  What a beautiful Pussy you are!"

Pussy said to the Owl, "You elegant fowl,
  How charmingly sweet you sing!
Oh! let us be married; too long we have tarried:
  But what shall we do for a ring?"
They sailed away, for a year and a day,
  To the land where the bong-tree grows;
And there in a wood a Piggy-wig stood,
  With a ring at the end of his nose,
      His nose,
      His nose,
  With a ring at the end of his nose.

"Dear Pig, are you willing to sell for one shilling
  Your ring?" Said the Piggy, "I will."
So they took it away, and were married next day
  By the turkey who lives on the hill.
They dined on mince and slices of quince,
  Which they ate with a runcible spoon;
And hand in hand, on the edge of the sand,
  They danced by the light of the moon,
      The moon,
      The moon,
  They danced by the light of the moon.

EDWARD LEAR

## LOW-ANCHORED CLOUD

Low-anchored cloud,
Newfoundland air,
Fountainhead and source of rivers,
Dew-cloth, dream drapery,
And napkin spread by fays;
Drifting meadow of the air,
Where bloom the daisied banks and violets,
And in whose fenny labyrinth
The bittern booms and heron wades;
Spirit of lakes and seas and rivers,
Bear only perfumes and the scent
Of healing herbs to just men's fields!

HENRY DAVID THOREAU

## HOPE

Hope was but a timid friend—
She sat without my grated den
Watching how my fate would tend
Even as selfish-hearted men.

She was cruel in her fear.
Through the bars, one dreary day,
I looked out to see her there
And she turned her face away!

Like a false guard false watch keeping
Still in strife she whispered peace;
She would sing while I was weeping,
If I listened, she would cease.

False she was, and unrelenting.
When my last joys stewed the ground
Even Sorrow saw repenting
Those sad relics scattered round;

Hope—whose whisper would have given
Balm to all that frenzied pain—
Stretched her wings and soared to heaven;
Went—and ne'er returned again!

EMILY BRONTË

## OUT OF THE CRADLE ENDLESSLY ROCKING

Out of the cradle endlessly rocking,
Out of the mocking-bird's throat, the musical shuttle,
Out of the Ninth-month midnight,
Over the sterile sands and the fields beyond, where the child leaving his bed wander'd alone, bareheaded, barefoot,
Down from the shower'd halo,
Up from the mystic play of shadows twining and twisting as if they were alive,
Out from the patches of briers and blackberries,
From the memories of the bird that chanted to me,
From your memories sad brother, from the fitful risings and fallings I heard,
From under that yellow half-moon late-risen and swollen as if with tears,
From those beginning notes of yearning and love there in the mist,
From the thousand responses of my heart never to cease,
From the myriad thence-arous'd words,
From the word stronger and more delicious than any,
From such as now they start the scene revisiting,
As a flock, twittering, rising, or overhead passing,
Borne hither, ere all eludes me, hurriedly,
A man, yet by these tears a little boy again,
Throwing myself on the sand, confronting the waves,
I, chanter of pains and joys, uniter of here and hereafter,
Taking all hints to use them, but swiftly leaping beyond them,
A reminiscence sing.

Once Paumanok,
When the lilac-scent was in the air and Fifth-month grass was growing,
Up this seashore in some briers,
Two feather'd guests from Alabama, two together,

And their nest, and four light-green eggs spotted with brown,
And every day the he-bird to and fro near at hand,
And every day the she-bird crouch'd on her nest, silent, with bright eyes,
And every day I, a curious boy, never too close, never disturbing them,
Cautiously peering, absorbing, translating.

*Shine! shine! shine!*
*Pour down your warmth, great sun!*
*While we bask, we two together.*

*Two together!*
*Winds blow south, or winds blow north,*
*Day come white, or night come black,*
*Home, or rivers and mountains from home,*
*Singing all time, minding no time,*
*While we two keep together.*

Till of a sudden,
May-be kill'd, unknown to her mate,
One forenoon the she-bird crouch'd not on the nest,
Nor return'd that afternoon, nor the next,
Nor ever appear'd again.

And thenceforward all summer in the sound of the sea,
And at night under the full of the moon in calmer weather,
Over the hoarse surging of the sea,
Or flitting from brier to brier by day,
I saw, I heard at intervals the remaining one, the he-bird,
The solitary guest from Alabama.

*Blow! blow! blow!*
*Blow up sea-winds along Paumanok's shore;*
*I wait and I wait till you blow my mate to me.*

Yes, when the stars glisten'd,
All night long on the prong of a moss-scallop'd stake,
Down almost amid the slapping waves,
Sat the lone singer wonderful causing tears.

He call'd on his mate,
He pour'd forth the meanings which I of all men know.

Yes my brother I know,
The rest might not, but I have treasur'd every note,
For more than once dimly down to the beach gliding,
Silent, avoiding the moonbeams, blending myself with the shadows,
Recalling now the obscure shapes, the echoes, the sounds and sights after their sorts,
The white arms out in the breakers tirelessly tossing,
I, with bare feet, a child, the wind wafting my hair,
Listen'd long and long.

Listen'd to keep, to sing, now translating the notes,
Following you my brother.

*Soothe! soothe! soothe!*
*Close on its wave soothes the wave behind,*
*And again another behind embracing and lapping, every one close,*
*But my love soothes not me, not me.*

*Low hangs the moon, it rose late,*
*It is lagging—O I think it is heavy with love, with love.*

*O madly the sea pushes upon the land,*
*With love, with love.*

*O night! do I not see my love fluttering out among the breakers?*
*What is that little black thing I see there in the white?*

Loud! loud! loud!
Loud I call to you, my love!

High and clear I shoot my voice over the waves,
Surely you must know who is here, is here,
You must know who I am, my love.

Low-hanging moon!
What is that dusky spot in your brown yellow?
O it is the shape, the shape of my mate!
O moon do not keep her from me any longer.

Land! land! O land!
Whichever way I turn, O I think you could give me my mate
back again if you only would,
For I am almost sure I see her dimly whichever way I look.

O rising stars!
Perhaps the one I want so much will rise, will rise with some
of you.

O throat! O trembling throat!
Sound clearer through the atmosphere!
Pierce the woods, the earth,
Somewhere listening to catch you must be the one I want.

Shake out carols!
Solitary here, the night's carols!
Carols of lonesome love! death's carols!

Carols under that lagging, yellow, waning moon!
O under that moon where she droops almost down into the
sea!
O reckless despairing carols.

But soft! sink low!
Soft! let me just murmur,
And do you wait a moment you husky-nois'd sea,
For somewhere I believe I heard my mate responding to me,
So faint, I must be still, be still to listen,
But not altogether still, for then she might not come immediately to me.

Hither my love!
Here I am! here!
With this just-sustain'd note I announce myself to you,
This gentle call is for you my love, for you.

Do not be decoy'd elsewhere,
That is the whistle of the wind, it is not my voice,
That is the fluttering, the fluttering of the spray,
Those are the shadows of leaves.

O darkness! O in vain!
O I am very sick and sorrowful.

O brown halo in the sky near the moon, drooping upon the sea!
O troubled reflection in the sea!
O throat! O throbbing heart!
And I singing uselessly, uselessly all the night.

O past! O happy life! O songs of joy!
In the air, in the woods, over fields,
Loved! loved! loved! loved! loved!
But my mate no more, no more with me!
We two together no more.

The aria sinking,
All else continuing, the stars shining,
The winds blowing, the notes of the bird continuous echoing,

With angry moans the fierce old mother incessantly
moaning,
On the sands of Paumanok's shore gray and rustling,
The yellow half-moon enlarged, sagging down, drooping,
the face of the sea almost touching,
The boy ecstatic, with his bare feet the waves, with his
hair the atmosphere dallying,
The love in the heart long pent, now loose, now at last
tumultuously bursting,
The aria's meaning, the ears, the soul, swiftly depositing,
The strange tears down the cheeks coursing,
The colloquy there, the trio, each uttering,
The undertone, the savage old mother incessantly crying,
To the boy's soul's questions sullenly timing, some drown'd
secret hissing,
To the outsetting bard.

Demon or bird! (said the boy's soul,)
Is it indeed toward your mate you sing? or is it really to me?
For I, that was a child, my tongue's use sleeping, now I
have heard you,
Now in a moment I know what I am for, I awake,
And already a thousand singers, a thousand songs, clearer,
louder and more sorrowful than yours,
A thousand warbling echoes have started to life within me,
never to die.

O you singer solitary, singing by yourself, projecting me,
O solitary me listening, never more shall I cease
perpetuating you,
Never more shall I escape, never more the reverberations,
Never more the cries of unsatisfied love be absent from me,
Never again leave me to be the peaceful child I was before
what there in the night,
By the sea under the yellow and sagging moon,
The messenger there arous'd, the fire, the sweet hell within,
The unknown want, the destiny of me.

O give me the clue! (it lurks in the night here somewhere,)
O if I am to have so much, let me have more!

A word then, (for I will conquer it,)
The word final, superior to all,
Subtle, sent up—what is it?—I listen;
Are you whispering it, and have been all the time, you
sea-waves?
Is that it from your liquid rims and wet sands?

Whereto answering, the sea,
Delaying not, hurrying not,
Whisper'd me through the night, and very plainly before
daybreak,
Lisp'd to me the low and delicious word death,
And again death, death, death, death,
Hissing melodious, neither like the bird nor like my
arous'd child's heart,
But edging near as privately for me rustling at my feet,
Creeping thence steadily up to my ears and laving me
softly all over,
Death, death, death, death, death.

Which I do not forget,
But fuse the song of my dusky demon and brother,
That he sang to me in the moonlight on Paumanok's
gray beach,

With the thousand responsive songs at random,
My own songs awaked from that hour,
And with them the key, the word up from the waves,
The word of the sweetest song and all songs,
That strong and delicious word which, creeping to my feet,
(Or like some old crone rocking the cradle, swathed
in sweet garments, bending aside,)
The sea whisper'd me.

WALT WHITMAN

## I HEAR AMERICA SINGING

I hear America singing, the varied carols I hear,
Those of mechanics, each one singing his as it should be blithe and strong,
The carpenter singing his as he measures his plank or beam,
The mason singing his as he makes ready for work, or leaves off work,
The boatman singing what belongs to him in his boat, the deck-hand singing on the steamboat deck,
The shoemaker singing as he sits on his bench, the hatter singing as he stands,
The wood-cutter's song, the plowboy's on his way in the morning, or at noon intermission or at sundown,
The delicious singing of the mother, or of the young wife at work, or of the girl sewing or washing,
Each singing what belongs to him or her and to none else,
The day what belongs to the day—at night the party of young fellows, robust, friendly,
Singing with open mouths their strong melodious songs.

WALT WHITMAN

## O CAPTAIN! MY CAPTAIN!

O Captain! my Captain! our fearful trip is done,
The ship has weathered every rack, the prize we sought is won,
The port is near, the bells I hear, the people all exulting,
While follow eyes the steady keel, the vessel grim and daring;
But O heart! heart! heart!
O the bleeding drops of red.
Where on the deck my Captain lies,
Fallen cold and dead.

O Captain! my Captain! rise up and hear the bells;
Rise up—for you the flag is hung—for you the bugle trills,
For you bouquets and ribboned wreaths—for you the shores a-crowding,
For you they call, the swaying mass, their eager faces turning;
Here Captain! dear father!
This arm beneath your head!
It is some dream that on the deck,
You've fallen cold and dead.

My Captain does not answer, his lips are pale and still,
My father does not feel my arm, he has no pulse nor will,
The ship is anchored safe and sound, its voyage closed and done,
From fearful trip the victor ship comes in with object won;
Exult, O shores, and ring, O bells!
But I with mournful tread,
Walk the deck my Captain lies,
Fallen cold and dead.

Walt Whitman

## I NEVER SAW A MOOR

I never saw a moor,
I never saw the sea;
Yet know I how the heather looks,
And what a wave must be.

I never spoke with God,
Nor visited in heaven;
Yet certain am I of the spot
As if the chart were given.

EMILY DICKINSON

## THE ONLY NEWS I KNOW

The only news I know
Is bulletins all day
From Immortality.

The only shows I see,
Tomorrow and Today,
Perchance Eternity.

The only One I meet
Is God,—the only street,
Existence; this traversed

If other news there be,
Or admirabler show—
I'll tell it you.

EMILY DICKINSON

## MY LIFE CLOSED TWICE

My life closed twice before its close—
It yet remains to see
If Immortality unveil
A third event to me

So huge, so hopeless to conceive
As these that twice befell.
Parting is all we know of heaven,
And all we need of hell.

EMILY DICKINSON

## THE SOUL SELECTS

The soul selects her own society,
Then shuts the door;
On her divine majority
Obtrude no more.

Unmoved, she notes the chariots pausing
At her low gate;
Unmoved, an emperor is kneeling
Upon her mat.

I've known her from an ample nation
Choose one;
Then close the valves of her attention
Like stone.

EMILY DICKINSON

## ECHO

Come to me in the silence of the night;
  Come in the sleeping silence of a dream;
Come with soft rounded cheeks and eyes as bright
  As sunlight on a stream;
    Come back in tears,
O memory, hope, love of finished years.

O dream how sweet, too sweet, too bitter sweet,
  Whose wakening should have been in Paradise,
Where souls brimful of love abide and meet;
  Where thirsting longful eyes
    Watch the slow door
That opening, letting in, lets out no more.

Yet come to me in dreams, that I may live
  My very life again though cold in death:
Come back to me in dreams, that I may give
  Pulse for pulse, breath for breath:
    Speak low, lean low,
As long ago, my love, how long ago.

CHRISTINA ROSSETTI

## FATHER WILLIAM

From *Alice in Wonderland*

"You are old, Father William," the young man said,
"And your hair has become very white;
And yet you incessantly stand on your head—
Do you think, at your age, it is right?"

"In my youth," Father William replied to his son,
"I feared it might injure the brain;
But, now that I'm perfectly sure I have none,
Why, I do it again and again."

"You are old," said the youth, "as I mentioned before,
And have grown most uncommonly fat;
Yet you turned a back-somersault in at the door—
Pray, what is the reason of that?"

"In my youth," said the sage, as he shook his gray locks,
"I kept all my limbs very supple
By the use of this ointment—one shilling the box—
Allow me to sell you a couple?"

"You are old," said the youth, "and your jaws are too
weak
For anything tougher than suet;
Yet you finished the goose, with the bones and the beak—
Pray, how did you manage to do it?"

"In my youth," said his father, "I took to the law,
And argued each case with my wife;
And the muscular strength which it gave to my jaw
Has lasted the rest of my life."

"You are old," said the youth, "one would hardly suppose
That your eye was as steady as ever;
Yet you balanced an eel on the end of your nose—
What made you so awfully clever?"

"I have answered three questions, and that is enough,"
Said his father. "Don't give yourself airs!
Do you think I can listen all day to such stuff?
Be off, or I'll kick you down-stairs!"

LEWIS CARROLL

# JABBERWOCKY

From *Through the Looking-Glass*

'Twas brillig, and the slithy toves
Did gyre and gimble in the wabe:
All mimsy were the borogoves,
And the mome raths outgrabe.

"Beware the Jabberwock, my son!
The jaws that bite, the claws that catch!
Beware the Jubjub bird, and shun
The frumious Bandersnatch!"

He took his vorpal sword in hand;
Long time the manxome foe he sought—
So rested he by the Tumtum tree,
And stood awhile in thought.

And, as in uffish thought he stood,
The Jabberwock, with eyes of flame,
Came whiffling through the tulgey wood,
And burbled as it came!

One, two! One, two! And through and through
The vorpal blade went snicker-snack!
He left it dead, and with its head
He went galumphing back.

"And hast thou slain the Jabberwock?
Come to my arms, my beamish boy!
O frabjous day! Callooh, Callay!"
He chortled in his joy.

'Twas brillig, and the slithy toves
Did gyre and gimble in the wabe:
All mimsy were the borogoves,
And the mome raths outgrabe.

LEWIS CARROLL

## THE DARKLING THRUSH

I leant upon a coppice gate
When Frost was specter-gray,
And Winter's dregs made desolate
The weakening eye of day.
The tangled bine-stems scored the sky
Like strings of broken lyres,
And all mankind that haunted nigh
Had sought their household fires.

The land's sharp features seemed to be
The Century's corpse outleant,
His crypt the cloudy canopy,
The wind his death-lament.
The ancient pulse of germ and birth
Was shrunken hard and dry,
And every spirit upon earth
Seemed fervorless as I.

At once a voice arose among
The bleak twigs overhead
In a full-hearted evensong
Of joy illimited;
An aged thrush, frail, gaunt, and small,
In blast-beruffled plume,
Had chosen thus to fling his soul
Upon the growing gloom.

So little cause for carolings
Of such ecstatic sound
Was written on terrestrial things
Afar or nigh around,
That I could think there trembled through
His happy good-night air
Some blessed Hope, whereof he knew
And I was unaware.

THOMAS HARDY

## INVICTUS

Out of the night that covers me,
Black as the Pit from pole to pole,
I thank whatever gods may be
For my unconquerable soul.

In the fell clutch of circumstance
I have not winced nor cried aloud.
Under the bludgeonings of chance
My head is bloody, but unbowed.

Beyond this place of wrath and tears
Looms but the horror of the shade,
And yet the menace of the years
Finds, and shall find me, unafraid.

It matters not how strait the gate,
How charged with punishments the scroll,
I am the master of my fate:
I am the captain of my soul.

WILLIAM ERNEST HENLEY

## SOLITUDE

Laugh, and the world laughs with you;
Weep, and you weep alone,
For the sad old earth must borrow its mirth,
But has trouble enough of its own.
Sing, and the hills will answer;
Sigh, it is lost on the air,
The echoes bound to a joyful sound,
But shrink from voicing care.

Rejoice, and men will seek you;
Grieve, and they turn and go.
They want full measure of all your pleasure,
But they do not need your woe
Be glad, and your friends are many;
Be sad, and you lose them all,—
There are none to decline your nectar'd wine,
But alone you must drink life's gall.

Feast, and your halls are crowded;
Fast, and the world goes by.
Succeed and give, and it helps you live,
But no man can help you die.
There is room in the halls of pleasure
For a large and lordly train,
But one by one we must all file on
Through the narrow aisles of pain.

Ella Wheeler Wilcox

## WHEN I WAS ONE-AND-TWENTY

When I was one-and-twenty
  I heard a wise man say,
"Give crowns and pounds and guineas
  But not your heart away;
Give pearls away and rubies
  But keep your fancy free."
But I was one-and-twenty,
  No use to talk to me.

When I was one-and-twenty
  I heard him say again,
"The heart out of the bosom
  Was never given in vain;
'Tis paid with sighs a plenty
  And sold for endless rue."
And I am two-and-twenty,
  And oh, 'tis true, 'tis true.

A. E. Houseman

## WITH RUE MY HEART IS LADEN

With rue my heart is laden
  For golden friends I had,
For many a rose-lipped maiden
  And many a lightfoot lad.

By brooks too broad for leaping
  The lightfoot boys are laid;
The rose-lipped girls are sleeping
  In fields where roses fade.

A. E. Houseman

EFB

## THE HOUND OF HEAVEN

I fled Him, down the nights and down the days;
I fled Him, down the arches of the years;
I fled Him, down the labyrinthine ways
Of my own mind; and in the mist of tears
I hid from Him, and under running laughter.
Up vistaed hopes I sped;
And shot, precipitated,
Adown Titanic glooms of chasmed fears,
From those strong Feet that followed, followed after.
But with unhurrying chase,
And unperturbéd pace,
Deliberate speed, majestic instancy,
They beat—and a Voice beat
More instant than the Feet—
"All things betray thee, who betrayest Me."
I pleaded, outlaw-wise,
By many a hearted casement, curtained red,
Trellised with intertwining charities
(For, though I knew His love Who followéd,
Yet was I sore adread
Lest, having Him, I must have naught beside);
But, if one little casement parted wide,
The gust of His approach would clash it to:
Fear wist not to evade, as Love wist to pursue.
Across the margent of the world I fled,
And troubled the gold gateways of the stars,
Smiting for shelter on their clanged bars;
Fretted to dulcet jars
And silvern chatter the pale ports o' the moon.
I said to Dawn: Be sudden—to Eve: Be soon;
With thy young skiey blossoms heap me over
From this tremendous Lover—
Float thy vague veil about me, lest He see!
I tempted all His servitors, but to find
My own betrayal in their constancy,
In faith to Him their fickleness to me,
Their traitorous tueness, and their loyal deceit.

To all swift things for swiftness did I sue;
Clung to the whistling mane of every wind.
But whether they swept, smoothly fleet,
The long savannahs of the blue;
Or whether, Thunder-driven,
They clanged his chariot 'thwart a heaven,
Plashy with flying lightnings round the spurn o' their feet:—
Fear wist not to evade as Love wist to pursue.
Still with unhurrying chase,
And unperturbéd pace,
Deliberate speed, majestic instancy,
Came on the following Feet,
And a Voice above their beat—
"Naught shelters thee, who wilt not shelter Me."

I sought no more that after which I strayed
In face of man or maid;
But still within the little children's eyes
Seems something, something that replies,
*They* at least are for me, surely for me!
I turned me to them very wistfully;
But just as their young eyes grew sudden fair
With dawning answers there,
Their angel plucked them from me by the hair.
"Come then, ye other children, Nature's—share
With me" (said I) "your delicate fellowship;
Let me greet you lip to lip,
Let me twine with you caresses,
Wantoning
With our Lady-Mother's vagrant tresses,
Banqueting
With her in her wind-walled palace,
Underneath her azured daïs,
Quaffing, as your taintless way is,
From a chalice
Lucent-weeping out of the dayspring."
So it was done:

*I* in their delicate fellowship was one—
Drew the bolt of Nature's secrecies.
    *I* knew all the swift importings
    On the willful face of skies;
    I knew how the clouds arise
    Spumed of the wild sea-snortings;
      All that's born or dies
      Rose and drooped with; made them shapers
Of mine own moods, or wailful or divine;
    With them joyed and was bereaven.
    I was heavy with the even,
    When she lit her glimmering tapers
    Round the day's dead sanctities.
    I laughed in the morning's eyes.
I triumphed and I saddened with all weather,
    Heaven and I wept together,
And its sweet tears were salt with mortal mine;

Against the red throb of its sunset-heart
    I laid my own to beat,
    And share commingling heat;
But not by that, by that, was eased my human smart.
In vain my tears were wet on Heaven's gray cheek.
For ah! we know not what each other says,
    These things and I; in sound *I* speak—
*Their* sound is but their stir, they speak by silences.
Nature, poor stepdame, cannot slake my drouth;
    Let her, if she would owe me,
Drop yon blue bosom-veil of sky, and show me
    The breasts o' her tenderness:
Never did any milk of hers once bless
      My thirsting mouth.
      Nigh and nigh draws the chase,
      With unperturbéd pace,
    Deliberate speed, majestic instancy;
      And past those noiséd Feet
      A Voice comes yet more fleet—
    "Lo! naught contents thee, who content'st not Me."

Naked I wait Thy love's uplifted stroke!
My harness piece by piece Thou hast hewn from me,
And smitten me to my knee;
I am defenseless utterly.
I slept, methinks, and woke,
And, slowly gazing, find me stripped in sleep.
In the rash lustihead of my young powers,
I shook the pillaring hours
And pulled my life upon me; grimed with smears,
I stand amid the dust o' the mounded years—
My mangled youth lies dead beneath the heap.
My days have crackled and gone up in smoke,
Have puffed and burst as sun-starts on a stream.
Yea, faileth now even dream
The dreamer, and the lute the lutanist;
Even the linked fantasies, in whose blossomy twist
I swung the earth a trinket at my wrist,
Are yielding; cords of all too weak account
For earth with heavy griefs so overplussed.
Ah! is Thy love indeed
A weed, albeit an amaranthine weed,
Suffering no flowers except its own to mount?
Ah! must—
Designer infinite!—
Ah! must Thou char the wood ere Thou canst limn
with it?
My freshness spent its wavering shower i' the dust;
And now my heart is as a broken fount,
Wherein tear-drippings stagnate, spilt down ever
From the dank thoughts that shiver
Upon the sighful branches of my mind.
Such is; what is to be?
The pulp so bitter, how shall taste the rind?
I dimly guess what Time in mist confounds;
Yet ever and anon a trumpet sounds
From the hid battlements of Eternity;
Those shaken mists a space unsettle, then
Round the half-glimpsed turrets slowly wash again.

But not ere him who summoneth
I first have seen, enwound
With glooming robes purpureal, cypress-crowned;
His name I know, and what his trumpet saith.
Whether man's heart or life it be which yields
Thee harvest, must Thy harvest-fields
Be dunged with rotten death?

Now of that long pursuit
Comes on at hand the bruit;
That Voice is round me like a bursting sea:
"And is thy earth so marred,
Shattered in shard on shard?
Lo, all things fly thee, for thou fliest Me!
Strange, piteous, futile thing!
Wherefore should any set thee love apart?
Seeing none but I makes much of naught" (He said),
"And human love needs human meriting:
How hast thou merited—
Of all man's clotted clay the dingiest clot?
Alack, thou knowest not
How little worthy of any love thou art!
Whom wilt thou find to love ignoble thee
Save Me, save only Me?
All which I took from thee I did but take,
Not for thy harms,
But just that thou might'st seek it in My arms.
All which thy child's mistake
Fancies as lost, I have stored for thee at home:
Rise, clasp My hand, and come!"
Halts by me that footfall:
Is my gloom, after all,
Shade of His hand, outstretched caressingly?
"Ah, fondest, blindest, weakest,
I am He Whom thou seekest!
Thou dravest love from thee, who dravest Me."

FRANCIS THOMPSON

## GUNGA DIN

You may talk o' gin an' beer
When you're quartered safe out 'ere,
An' you're sent to penny-fights an' Aldershot it;
But if it comes to slaughter
You will do your work on water,
An' you'll lick the bloomin' boots of 'im that's got it.
Now in Injia's sunny clime,
Where I used to spend my time
A-servin' of 'Er Majesty the Queen,
Of all them black-faced crew
The finest man I knew
Was our regimental *bhisti,* Gunga Din.
        He was "Din! Din! Din!
        You limping lump o' brick-dust, Gunga Din!
        Hi! *slippy hitherao!*
        Water, get it! *Hanee lao!*
        You squidgy-nosed old idol, Gunga Din!"

The uniform 'e wore
Was nothin' much before,
An' rather less than 'arf o' that be'ind,
For a twisty piece o' rag
An' a goatskin water bag
Was all the field-equipment 'e could find.
When the sweatin' troop-train lay
In a sidin' through the day,
Where the 'eat would make your bloomin' eye-brows crawl,
We shouted "Harry By!"
Till our throats were bricky-dry,
Then we wopped 'im 'cause 'e couldn't serve us all.
        It was "Din! Din! Din!
        You 'eathen, where the mischief 'ave you been?
        You put some *juldee* in it,
        Or I'll *marrow* you this minute
        If you don't fill up my helmet, Gunga Din!"

'E would dot an' carry one
Till the longest day was done,
An' 'e didn't seem to know the use o' fear.
If we charged or broke or cut,
You could bet your bloomin' nut,
'E'd be waitin' fifty paces right flank rear.
With 'is *mussick* on 'is back,
'E would skip with our attack,
An' watch us till the bugles made "Retire."
An' for all 'is dirty 'ide
'E was white, clear white, inside
When 'e went to tend the wounded under fire!
    It was "Din! Din! Din!"
    With the bullets kickin' dust-spots on the green.
    When the cartridges ran out,
    You could 'ear the front-files shout:
    "Hi! ammunition-mules an' Gunga Din!"

I sha'n't forgit the night
When I dropped be'ind the fight
With a bullet where my belt-plate should 'a' been.
I was chokin' mad with thirst,
An' the man that spied me first
Was our good old grinnin', gruntin' Gunga Din.
'E lifted up my 'ead,
An' 'e plugged me where I bled,
An' 'e guv me 'arf-a-pint o' water—green:
It was crawlin' and it stunk,
But of all the drinks I've drunk,
I'm gratefullest to one from Gunga Din.
    It was "Din! Din! Din!
    'Ere's a beggar with a bullet through 'is spleen;
    'E's chawin' up the ground an' 'e's kickin' all around:
    For Gawd's sake git the water, Gunga Din!"

'E carried me away
To where a *dooli* lay,
An' a bullet come an' drilled the beggar clean.
'E put me safe inside,
An' just before 'e died:
"I 'ope you liked your drink," sez Gunga Din.
So I'll meet 'im later on
In the place where 'e is gone,
Where it's always double drill and no canteen;
'E'll be squattin' on the coals
Givin' drinks to pore damned souls,
An' I'll get a swig in Hell from Gunga Din!
        Din! Din! Din!
        You Lazarushian-leather Gunga Din!
        Tho I've belted you an' flayed you,
        By the livin' Gawd that made you,
        You're a better man than I am, Gunga Din!

RUDYARD KIPLING

## THE LAKE ISLE OF INNISFREE

I will arise and go now, and go to Innisfree,
And a small cabin build there, of clay and wattles made;
Nine bean rows will I have there, a hive for the honey bee,
And live alone in the bee-loud glade.

And I shall have some peace there, for peace comes dropping slow,
Dropping from the veils of the morning to where the cricket sings;
There midnight's all a glimmer, and noon a purple glow,
And evening full of the linnet's wings.

I will arise and go now, for always night and day
I hear lake water lapping with low sounds by the shore;
While I stand on the roadway, or on the pavements gray,
I hear it in the deep heart's core.

William Butler Yeats

## THE SORROW OF LOVE

The quarrel of the sparrows in the eaves,
The full round moon and the star-laden sky,
And the loud song of the ever-singing leaves
Had hid away earth's old and weary cry.

And then you came with those red mournful lips,
And with you came the whole of the world's tears,
And all the sorrows of her labouring ships,
And all the burden of her myriad years.

And now the sparrows warring in the eaves,
The curd-pale moon, the white stars in the sky,
And the loud chanting of the unquiet leaves,
Are shaken with earth's old and weary cry.

WILLIAM BUTLER YEATS

# CYNARA

*Non sum qualis eram bonae sub regno Cynarae*

Last night, ah, yesternight, betwixt her lips and mine
There fell thy shadow, Cynara! thy breath was shed
Upon my soul between the kisses and the wine;
And I was desolate and sick of an old passion,
  Yea, I was desolate and bowed my head:
I have been faithful to thee, Cynara! in my fashion.

All night upon mine heart I felt her warm heart beat,
Night-long within mine arms in love and sleep she lay;
Surely the kisses of her bought red mouth were sweet;
But I was desolate and sick of an old passion,
  When I awoke and found the dawn was gray:
I have been faithful to thee, Cynara! in my fashion.

I have forgot much, Cynara! gone with the wind,
Flung roses, roses riotously with the throng,
Dancing, to put thy pale, lost lilies out of mind;
But I was desolate and sick of an old passion,
  Yea, all the time, because the dance was long:
I have been faithful to thee, Cynara! in my fashion.

I cried for madder music and for stronger wine,
But when the feast is finished and the lamps expire,
Then falls thy shadow, Cynara! the night is thine;
And I am desolate and sick of an old passion,
  Yea, hungry for the lips of my desire:
I have been faithful to thee, Cynara! in my fashion.

ERNEST DOWSON

## MINIVER CHEEVY

Miniver Cheevy, child of scorn,
  Grew lean while he assailed the seasons;
He wept that he was ever born,
  And he had reasons.

Miniver loved the days of old
  When swords were bright and steeds were prancing;
The vision of a warrior bold
  Would set him dancing.

Miniver sighed for what was not,
  And dreamed, and rested from his labors;
He dreamed of Thebes and Camelot,
  And Priam's neighbors.

Miniver mourned the ripe renown
  That made so many a name so fragrant;
He mourned Romance, now on the town,
  And Art, a vagrant.

Miniver loved the Medici,
  Albeit he had never seen one;
He would have sinned incessantly
  Could he have been one.

Miniver cursed the commonplace
  And eyed a khaki suit with loathing;
He missed the medieval grace
  Of iron clothing.

Miniver scorned the gold he sought,
  But sore annoyed was he without it;
Miniver thought, and thought, and thought,
  And thought about it.

Miniver Cheevy, born too late,
  Scratched his head and kept on thinking;
Miniver coughed, and called it fate,
  And kept on drinking.

EDWIN ARLINGTON ROBINSON

## MENDING WALL

Something there is that doesn't love a wall,
That sends the frozen-ground-swell under it
And spills the upper boulders in the sun,
And makes gaps even two can pass abreast.
The work of hunters is another thing:
I have come after them and made repair
Where they have left not one stone on a stone,
But they would have the rabbit out of hiding,
To please the yelping dogs. The gaps I mean,
No one has seen them made or heard them made,
But at spring mending-time we find them there.
I let my neighbor know beyond the hill;
And on a day we meet to walk the line
And set the wall between us once again.
We keep the wall between us as we go.
To each the boulders that have fallen to each.
And some are loaves and some so nearly balls
We have to use a spell to make them balance:
"Stay where you are until our backs are turned!"
We wear our fingers rough with handling them.
Oh, just another kind of out-door game,
One on a side. It comes to little more:
There where it is we do not need the wall:
He is all pine and I am apple orchard.
My apple trees will never get across
And eat the cones under his pines, I tell him.
He only says, "Good fences make good neighbors."
Spring is the mischief in me, and I wonder
If I could put a notion in his head:
*"Why* do they make good neighbors? Isn't it
Where there are cows? But here there are no cows.
Before I built a wall I'd ask to know
What I was walling in or walling out,
And to whom I was like to give offense.
Something there is that doesn't love a wall,
That wants it down." I could say "Elves" to him,

But it's not elves exactly, and I'd rather
He said it for himself. I see him there,
Bringing a stone grasped firmly by the top
In each hand, like an old-stone savage armed.
He moves in darkness as it seems to me,
Not of woods only and the shade of trees.
He will not go behind his father's saying,
And he likes having thought of it so well
He says again, "Good fences make good neighbors."

ROBERT FROST

## THE ROAD NOT TAKEN

Two roads diverged in a yellow wood,
And sorry I could not travel both
And be one traveler, long I stood
And looked down one as far as I could
To where it bent in the undergrowth;

Then took the other, as just as fair,
And having perhaps the better claim,
Because it was grassy and wanted wear;
Though as for that the passing there
Had worn them really about the same,

And both that morning equally lay
In leaves no step had trodden black.
Oh, I kept the first for another day!
Yet knowing how way leads on to way,
I doubted if I should ever come back.

I shall be telling this with a sigh
Somewhere ages and ages hence:
Two roads diverged in a wood, and I—
I took the one less traveled by,
And that has made all the difference.

ROBERT FROST

## BIRCHES

When I see birches bend to left and right
Across the lines of straighter darker trees,
I like to think some boy's been swinging them.
But swinging doesn't bend them down to stay
As ice-storms do. Often you must have seen them
Loaded with ice a sunny winter morning
After a rain. They click upon themselves
As the breeze rises, and turn many-colored
As the stir cracks and crazes their enamel.
Soon the sun's warmth makes them shed crystal shells
Shattering and avalanching on the snowcrust—
Such heaps of broken glass to sweep away
You'd think the inner dome of heaven had fallen.
They are dragged to the withered bracken by the load,
And they seem not to break; though once they are bowed
So low for long, they never right themselves:
You may see their trunks arching in the woods
Years afterwards, trailing their leaves on the ground
Like girls on hands and knees that throw their hair
Before them over their heads to dry in the sun.
But I was going to say when Truth broke in
With all her matter of fact about the ice-storm,
I should prefer to have some boy bend them
As he went out and in to fetch the cows—
Some boy too far from town to learn baseball,
Whose only play was what he found himself,
Summer or winter, and could play alone.
One by one he subdued his father's trees
By riding them down over and over again
Until he took the stiffness out of them,

And not one but hung limp, not one was left
For him to conquer. He learned all there was
To learn about not launching out too soon
And so not carrying the tree away
Clear to the ground. He always kept his poise
To the top branches, climbing carefully
With the same pains you use to fill a cup
Up to the brim, and even above the brim.
Then he flung outward, feet first, with a swish,
Kicking his way down through the air to the ground.
So was I once myself a swinger of birches.
And so I dream of going back to be.
It's when I'm weary of considerations,
And life is too much like a pathless wood
Where your face burns and tickles with the cobwebs
Broken across it, and one eye is weeping
From a twig's having lashed across it open.
I'd like to get away from earth awhile
And then come back to it and begin over.
May no fate willfully misunderstand me
And half grant what I wish and snatch me away
Not to return. Earth's the right place for love:
I don't know where it's likely to go better.
I'd like to go by climbing a birch tree,
And climb black branches up a snow-white trunk
*Toward* heaven, till the tree could bear no more,
But dipped its top and set me down again.
That would be good both going and coming back.
One could do worse than be a swinger of birches.

ROBERT FROST

## CHICAGO

Hog Butcher for the World,
Tool Maker, Stacker of Wheat,
Player with Railroads and the Nation's Freight Handler;
Stormy, husky, brawling,
City of the Big Shoulders:

They tell me you are wicked and I believe them, for I have seen your painted women under the gas lamps luring the farm boys.
And they tell me you are crooked and I answer: Yes, it is true I have seen the gunman kill and go free to kill again.
And they tell me you are brutal and my reply is: On the faces of women and children I have seen the marks of wanton hunger.
And having answered so I turn once more to those who sneer at this my city, and I give them back the sneer and say to them:
Come and show me another city and lifted head singing so proud to be alive and coarse and strong and cunning.
Flinging magnetic curses amid the toil of piling job on job, here is a tall bold slugger set vivid against the little soft cities;
Fierce as a dog with tongue lapping for action, cunning as a savage pitted against the wilderness,
Bareheaded,
Shoveling,
Wrecking,
Planning,
Building, breaking, rebuilding,
Under the smoke, dust all over his mouth, laughing with white teeth,
Under the terrible burden of destiny laughing as a young man laughs,

Laughing even as an ignorant fighter laughs who has
never lost a battle,
Bragging and laughing that under his wrist is the pulse,
and under his ribs the heart of the people,
Laughing!
Laughing the stormy, husky, brawling laughter of Youth,
half-naked, sweating, proud to be Hog Butcher, Tool
Maker, Stacker of Wheat, Player with Railroads and
Freight Handler to the Nation.

CARL SANDBURG

## FOG

The fog comes
on little cat feet.

It sits looking
over harbor and city
on silent haunches
and then moves on.

CARL SANDBURG

## TREES

*For Mrs. Henry Mills Alden*

I think that I shall never see
A poem lovely as a tree.

A tree whose hungry mouth is prest
Against the earth's sweet flowing breast;
A tree that looks at God all day,
And lifts her leafy arms to pray;

A tree that may in Summer wear
A nest of robins in her hair;

Upon whose bosom snow has lain;
Who intimately lives with rain.

Poems are made by fools like me,
But only God can make a tree.

JOYCE KILMER